MW00958993

Emotional Vulnerability in Men

Finding Strength in Sensitivity to
Navigate Relationships, Work,
Fatherhood, and Modern Masculinity

Richard Garraway

© **Copyright 2024 Richard Garraway All rights reserved.**

The content contained within this book may not be reproduced, duplicated or transmitted without direct written permission from the author or the publisher.

Under no circumstances will any blame or legal responsibility be held against the publisher, or author, for any damages, reparation, or monetary loss due to the information contained within this book, either directly or indirectly.

Legal Notice:

This book is copyright protected. It is only for personal use. You cannot amend, distribute, sell, use, quote or paraphrase any part, or the content within this book, without the consent of the author or publisher.

Disclaimer Notice:

Please note the information contained within this document is for educational and entertainment purposes only. All effort has been executed to present accurate, up to date, reliable, complete information. No warranties of any kind are declared or implied. Readers acknowledge that the author is not engaged in the rendering of legal, financial, medical or professional advice. The content within this book has been derived from various sources. Please consult a licensed professional before attempting any techniques outlined in this book.

By reading this document, the reader agrees that under no circumstances is the author responsible for any losses, direct or indirect, that are incurred as a result of the use of the information contained within this document, including, but not limited to, errors, omissions, or inaccuracies.

Table of Contents

YOUR FREE GIFT

As a special thank you, I'm delighted to offer you a free gift
Introducing **"Your Emotional Intelligence Quiz"**

To claim your free gift and embark on this life-changing journey, visit:

https://richardgarrawaybooks.com/Free-Gift-7

Why take the quiz?

Gain Self-Awareness: Identify emotional strengths and growth areas to improve relationships, and communication.

Discover Your Emotional Intelligence Level: *Level 1: Exploring Emotional Awareness,* **Level 2:** *Embracing Emotional Growth,* **Level 3:** *Cultivating Emotional Balance,* **Level 4:** *Mastering Emotional Intelligence,* **Level 5:** *Elevating Emotional Mastery*

Personalized Guidance: Get custom feedback and actionable steps to boost emotional intelligence and personal growth.

Empowerment: Start enhancing your emotional skills for resilience and grace.

Direction: Set clear goals for improved emotional intelligence, leading to greater life fulfillment

Thank you for your support and trust in "Emotional Vulnerability in Men."

Richard Garraway.

Introduction

My son, barely eight years old, sat beside me, tears welling in his eyes. It was sports day at his elementary school. My son was in the baseball competition. I had seen him practice over the past few weeks, and he had been so excited about it, so I decided to be there to encourage him. His little face would light up. He swung the plastic bat, imagining hitting home runs like one of his favourite players.

The other kids lined up on the makeshift field. Their sneakers scuffed the grass. My son stood there, clutching the bat. He was so determined to win the game for his team.

His uniform was slightly too big for him, the cap slipping down over his eyes. But he didn't care; he was ready to give it his all.

As the game progressed, it became evident that victory wasn't on the cards for him. Despite his best efforts, the opposing team seemed to outshine him at every turn. The ball flew through the air, and my heart raced alongside it. I watched as my son swung, his small frame twisting with effort. But the ball sailed past him, and the disappointment in his eyes was palpable.

Then it happened—the final pitch, the decisive moment that sealed his team's loss.

As he left the pitch and walked to me, I felt pressure to be the "strong dad." I should offer a stoic pat on the back and a quick "good game." But this time, something felt different. As he reached the dugout, I kneeled, meeting his tear-filled eyes.

"Hey, champ," I said, my voice thick with emotion. "That was a tough game. You fought hard out there."

He sniffled, surprise flickering across his face. "We lost," he mumbled, kicking at a clump of dirt.

I smiled, a genuine one that warmed my own heart. "Yeah, we did. But you know what? Sometimes even the best teams lose."

His eyes widened as I continued, "The real win is how you played the game. Did you give it your all? Did you have fun?"

He hesitated for a moment, then a small smile tugged at the corners of his lips. "Yeah, I guess."

"That's what matters," I said, pulling him into a hug.

The warmth of his small body pressed against mine. At that moment, I realized my true strength. It wasn't about stoicism. It was about vulnerability. It was about acknowledging emotions. And, it was about creating a safe space for your child to do the same. He needed a hug. He also needed a word of encouragement and a shared moment of vulnerability. These things were more important than the outcome of the game. Taking a deep breath, I reached out and pulled my son into a tight embrace. "That's okay, champ," I whispered, my voice thick with emotion. "We'll practice together this week.

The rest of the day unfolded with cheers and laughter. We watched other games, shared snacks, and even got our faces painted with team colors.

The story you just read exemplifies the internal struggle men face.

Vulnerability isn't weakness; it is our bridge to authenticity. Maybe we could embrace it. Then, we could rewrite the rules of masculinity. We could create a world where tears show resilience, not defeat.

In the past, masculinity has meant stoicism and strength. Men have been conditioned to believe that vulnerability is weakness, a chink in our armour that exposes us to ridicule and rejection. But the reality is far more complex.

The modern landscape for men is a shifting one. Societal expectations are changing slowly. But the pressure to conform to old ideas of masculinity remains. We juggle careers, relationships, and families, all while navigating a constant double bind. Be strong and stoic, and be the rock. But also, be emotionally available, be a supportive partner, and be a present father. These seemingly contradictory expectations can leave us feeling isolated and confused.

Many men experience a constant internal battle. We want to connect with our loved ones and express our emotions openly, but the fear of judgment holds us back. We bottle up our feelings. This leads to emotional detachment and a disconnect from ourselves and those around us. This hidden struggle manifests in various ways – difficulty expressing anger or sadness, emotional withdrawal in relationships, and even struggles with mental health.

Vulnerability is not a flaw to be hidden, but a strength to be embraced.

In "Emotional Vulnerability in Men", we will break these walls and forge a path towards a more fulfilling life. Here, we'll tackle the complexities of emotional vulnerability head-on. We'll explore the concepts behind emotions, debunking the myth that expressing them diminishes our masculinity. We need to shift from the dynamics of societal expectations to dissecting traditional norms and exploring their impact on our emotional well-being in the modern world.

This is more than just a book; it's an invitation. An invitation to embark on a progressive journey of self-discovery. You will learn strategies for navigating difficult conversations. They will help you connect better with your partner and children. You will also learn to express your emotional needs in a healthy manner. This will help you become stronger.

This book stands as a beacon of guidance and empowerment. **As you read this book, it will help you:**

1. Understand the complexities of emotional vulnerability in men and how societal norms impact our ability to express and navigate our emotions authentically.

2. Recognize the hidden struggles you may face when navigating emotional expression, and provide you with tools to overcome these obstacles.

3. Embrace your full emotional spectrum by discovering how to acknowledge and express all your emotions, from joy and love to anger and sadness, healthily and authentically.

4. Challenge the pervasive societal norms and expectations that pressure men to conform to stoic expressions of strength and empower you to embrace vulnerability as a source of authenticity and resilience.

5. Building stronger relationships with the power of vulnerability to cultivate deeper connections with friends, family, and partners.

6. Thrive in the workplace by cultivating emotional intelligence, resilience, authenticity, and breaking free from the constraints of traditional masculinity.

7. Embrace fatherhood and parenting with empathy, understanding, and emotional openness, creating a nurturing and supportive environment for your children to flourish.

8. Cultivate a sense of community and connection with like-minded individuals who are also on a journey of self-discovery and authenticity.

9. Create a personal growth blueprint tailored to your unique journey, empowering you to live a more fulfilling and authentic life.

10. Creating a more fulfilling life by discovering the power of emotional vulnerability to build a life that is richer, more meaningful, and filled with deeper connections

I am not just the author of this book. I bring expertise in navigating vulnerability. I also understand the challenges men face. Together, we can find ourselves. We can learn the strategies to emerge stronger, more real, and truly empowered. I am also on this journey with you. I've been able to break this barrier, and I understand your struggles and believe unequivocally in your ability to overcome them.

Perhaps you're wondering, "Who am I to guide you on this journey?" As the author of this book, I've spent years exploring the complexities of masculinity and emotional vulnerability. I have seen the power of embracing our true selves. I saw it through my experience and research. My goal is to be your trusted companion on this path, offering insights, support, and the tools you need to thrive.

By the time you turn the final page, you won't just understand the challenges of emotional vulnerability in men; you'll be equipped to navigate them.

I am an individual with an unwavering passion for empowering men on their journey toward emotional vulnerability. I was fueled by a deep commitment. I wanted to break down societal norms and foster authenticity. I channeled this passion into writing this book.

Each person's journey is unique. This book gives tailored guidance, not generic advice. You will learn from a mix of psychology, exercises, and stories. The tools are made for your challenges.

Are you ready to accept your vulnerability? Doing so unlocks the power to build deeper connections and gain self-awareness. It also lets you forge a path to a richer life of purpose and fulfilment. It's time to embrace our emotions, share our stories, and rewrite the rules of masculinity. Turn the page and embark on a journey of emotional liberation. It's time to break the barriers.

Part 1: Unmasking Emotions - Recognizing and Embracing Vulnerability in Relationships

Chapter 1: The Hidden Struggle

Is vulnerability the same as weakness? We often link vulnerability with emotions we do not want to feel, like fear, shame, and uncertainty. However, we overlook that vulnerability is also where joy, creativity, authenticity, and love originate.

Our society has woven men into a rigid pattern of

stoicism, toughness, and emotional restraint. From a young age, a boy is taught to suppress his emotions and bury his vulnerabilities beneath his strength; if not, he will be seen as weak. Gradually, a hidden struggle, an internal conflict that festers in the shadows of masculinity, begins to surface.

Society often tells men to "man up" and bottle up their feelings. But emotions are a natural part of life, and pushing them down can be harmful. It can lead to feeling isolated, disconnected from loved ones, and even struggling with mental health.

Vulnerability isn't weakness. It's a strength. It takes courage to open up about what you're feeling, and it can lead to deeper connections with others. Being able to truly share your joys and sorrows with the people you care about is the power of emotional vulnerability.

This chapter delves into the invisible war men wage within themselves. In our exploration, we'll focus on the societal expectations that dictate traditional masculinity, highlighting the pressure to suppress emotions and maintain invulnerability. We'll look at the role of the media. We'll also look at family dynamics and cultural backgrounds. They shape these expectations. We'll also explore the psychological effects of emotional suppression. We'll look at the fear of judgment and the inner conflict. This conflict arises from wanting authenticity while fearing rejection. I will show you practical examples. You will learn to admit and handle these hidden struggles. This will pave the way for a journey of self-discovery and openness.

Societal Expectation

Societal expectations often cast men as the embodiment of traditional masculinity. Society has long prescribed a narrow definition of masculinity. It's like a script that dictates how men should behave, think, and, above all, feel. Many see stoicism, toughness, and restraint as the cornerstones of being a "real man."" But where did this script come from, and how is it affecting men today?

Traditional Masculinity

The pressure to conform to traditional ideas of masculinity can harm men's mental health and emotions.

Psychologists have long argued that suppressing emotions is not healthy. Studies by James Gross of Stanford University show that hiding emotions causes more stress. It also causes anxiety and health problems. Imagine a pressure cooker; the longer you keep the heat on without releasing the steam, the more likely it is to explode. The same principle applies to our emotions. When we don't healthily express them, they can build up and eventually erupt in unhealthy ways, like anger outbursts or withdrawal.

Media Influence

The media plays a significant role in shaping societal expectations of masculinity. Men are often shown this way in media, from movies to ads. These representations reinforce the idea that vulnerability is a sign of weakness, perpetuating harmful stereotypes and making it difficult for men to express their emotions openly.

A study published in the journal Sex Roles revealed that exposure to traditional masculine media messages is indeed associated with negative attitudes toward seeking help for mental health issues among men. The research highlights how adherence to masculine norms can impact men's mental health and their willingness to seek psychological assistance. It's essential to recognize and address these societal influences to promote better mental well-being for everyone.

These media portrayals reinforce the notion that vulnerability is a sign of weakness. The message is clear: real men don't cry, they conquer.

Research by the American Psychological Association (APA) suggests that men experience a full range of emotions, just like women. The difference lies not in the feeling itself but in how we're conditioned to express it.

Family and Cultural Upbringing

Family dynamics and cultural backgrounds also play a significant role in shaping men's attitudes toward emotional expression. In many households, boys are socialized to conform to traditional gender roles, with girls encouraged to be nurturing and emotional while boys are taught to be strong and stoic. This can create a sense of pressure for boys to suppress their emotions and conform to societal expectations of masculinity.

Cultural norms and traditions can further reinforce these expectations, making it challenging for men to break free from traditional gender roles. In some cultures, showing vulnerability or expressing emotions openly is seen as a sign of weakness, leading men to internalize these beliefs and hide their true feelings from others.

In conclusion, societal expectations of masculinity place a heavy burden on men, forcing them to conform to narrow ideals of strength and toughness while suppressing their emotions. This pressure to succumb to traditional norms can have negative consequences for men's mental and emotional well-being, contributing to feelings of isolation, loneliness, and emotional distress.

Unraveling the Emotional Suppression

Suppressing emotions may seem like a coping mechanism, but the psychological effect it has on men is profound.

Psychological Impact

Burying feelings can cause stress, anxiety, and depression. Suppressing emotions doesn't make them disappear. Instead, they fester, causing mental health issues.

Consider holding up a bottle of water; it feels weightless and effortless to hold. Imagine keeping it raised for a minute. Now, picture holding it for an entire hour. Over time, that weightless bottle would become unbearable. You might experience pain and even lose feeling in your arm. This reflects the impact of suppressing emotions. At first, it might seem inconsequential. Continuing to bottle up feelings over time causes emotional weight to accumulate. This turns a small burden into a source of pain.

Numerous studies have linked emotional suppression to adverse effects on mental health. Individuals who habitually suppress emotions experience higher psychological distress levels. The American Psychological Association says hidden emotions can cause physical problems like headaches and digestive issues. These issues might also lead to cardiovascular problems.

Fear of Judgment

But why do men continue to suppress their emotions despite the toll it takes on their mental health? One major factor is the fear of judgment. From a young age, men are taught to be strong, resilient, and unflappable. Expressing vulnerability is often equated with weakness, leaving men feeling vulnerable to ridicule, rejection, and shame.

The fear of judgment can come from both external sources and self-imposed expectations. Men may worry about how their friends, family, or colleagues will perceive them if they show any signs of emotional vulnerability. They may fear that opening up about their struggles will make them appear less capable.

But the fear doesn't always come from external sources. Sometimes, the biggest critic is the voice inside our heads. This inner critic might tell you that your emotions are "unmanly" or "unworthy" of being shared. This self-judgment can be just as debilitating as the fear of external judgment.

Breaking the Cycle: From Concealment to Connection

While suppressing emotions might seem like a way to protect yourself, it ultimately hinders your well-being. The good news is that you can break free from this cycle. Here are some tips:

1. Acknowledge Your Emotions: The first step is to become aware of your emotions. Pay attention to what you're feeling throughout the day, both positive and negative.

2. Challenge Negative Self-Talk: When your inner critic starts whispering doubts, challenge those thoughts. Remind yourself it's okay to feel different emotions. Expressing them shows strength, not weakness.

3. Start Small: Don't feel pressured to open up about everything at once. Start by sharing a small vulnerability with a trusted fellow

Seeking support from trusted friends, family members, or a therapist can also help alleviate the fear of judgment. Vulnerability is a shared human experience. Sharing struggles can bring empathy and connection.

Internal Conflict and Isolation

Internal Struggles

Many men silently battle between societal expectations and authentic emotional expression. The battle can lead to isolation. You may feel disconnected from yourself and others.

Society often sends a mixed message. On the one hand, men are expected to be strong, stoic figures, providers, and protectors. On the other hand, there's a growing awareness of the importance of mental health, encouraging everyone to express their emotions. This creates a confusing double bind for men – wanting to be seen as strong while also desiring emotional connection and vulnerability.

Isolation and Loneliness

Men who struggle with emotional vulnerability often feel isolated and lonely. This intensifies their internal conflict. Suppressing emotions and isolating ourselves creates barriers to connecting authentically with others. We may put up walls, keeping people at arm's length, to avoid the risk of being seen as weak or vulnerable.

Our efforts to protect ourselves end up isolating us more. We miss the chance for real connection by not sharing vulnerabilities. Sharing vulnerabilities creates intimacy and support. Instead of finding solace in solitude, we find ourselves trapped in a cycle of loneliness, longing for connection but unsure of how to break free from our self-imposed isolation.

Research underscores the detrimental effects of loneliness on mental and physical health. Loneliness is linked to various health issues. These include depression, anxiety, and cardiovascular disease. Loneliness also increases the risk of premature death. Loneliness takes a toll. It's crucial to address emotional struggles and build meaningful connections.

So how do we break free from the cycle of isolation and loneliness? It starts with vulnerability. Courageously share your struggles with trusted individuals. This helps break down barriers that isolate us. Vulnerability helps build authentic connections based on empathy, understanding, and mutual support.

Taboo Surrounding Vulnerability

We discussed men's internal conflict and societal pressure. Yet the struggle with vulnerability goes beyond individual experiences. There are deeper cultural norms and unspoken rules that create a significant barrier to men expressing their emotions openly.

Imagine you're visiting a new country with a completely different culture. Their customs, greetings, and social interactions may confuse you. There are unspoken rules, a cultural code that dictates behaviour. Unfortunately, men often face taboos about expressing emotions. This taboo involves vulnerability.

Cultural Barriers

Many cultures deeply embed male vulnerability in societal norms. From a young age, parents and society often instill in male children the expectation to be tough, stoic, and emotionally resilient. Any display of vulnerability is viewed as a sign of weakness, eliciting ridicule or dismissal. This cultural conditioning creates a barrier to open conversations about emotions, leaving many men feeling isolated and unable to express their true feelings.

Research shows that cultural norms strongly influence attitudes toward male vulnerability. Studies show that in cultures emphasizing traditional gender roles, men are less likely to seek help for emotional issues. They are also more likely to conform to traditional masculine norms. Rigid gender roles impact men's mental health and relationships. This adherence also affects their overall well-being.

Impact on Relationships

Struggling with vulnerability can deeply impact relationships, both romantic and platonic. In romantic relationships, not expressing emotions openly can cause communication breakdowns and a lack of intimacy. Partners may feel disconnected and struggle to understand each other's emotional needs. They may find it challenging to provide support.

Moreover, the taboo surrounding vulnerability can create power imbalances within relationships. One partner unable to express emotions may burden the other with providing support without reciprocation. This imbalance can strain the relationship and lead to resentment or dissatisfaction.

In platonic relationships, the impact of the hidden struggle with vulnerability is equally significant. Friendships may suffer when men feel unable to share their true feelings with their friends. This lack of emotional connection can lead to shallow or superficial relationships, leaving men feeling isolated and misunderstood.

Practical Advice

To overcome cultural barriers and taboos on vulnerability, you need courage and self-awareness. Here are some practical steps you can take to navigate these challenges:

1. Challenge Gender Stereotypes: Question traditional notions of masculinity and challenge societal expectations that dictate men should be emotionally stoic. Embrace the idea that vulnerability is a strength, not a weakness.

2. Create a safe environment. Encourage open conversations about emotions. Practice active listening and validate each other's feelings without judgment.

3. Seek support: Be bold and reach out for help when needed. Whether it's talking to a trusted friend, seeking therapy, or

joining a support group, seeking support can help you navigate the challenges of vulnerability.

4. Cultivate Empathy: Practice empathy towards yourself and others. Understand that vulnerability is a universal human experience and that showing compassion towards yourself and others can help break down barriers and foster deeper connections.

By challenging cultural barriers and embracing vulnerability, you can create more authentic and fulfilling relationships, both romantically and platonically.

Action Plan for Empowering Emotional Vulnerability

Reflective Exercises

To begin your journey towards embracing emotional vulnerability, take some time to reflect on your personal experiences with emotional suppression. Find a quiet space where you can be alone with your thoughts, and consider the following questions:

1. What societal expectations or cultural norms have influenced my views on masculinity and emotional expression?

2. How have I experienced the pressure to conform to traditional ideas of masculinity, and how has this impacted my ability to authenticate my emotions?

3. Can I identify any specific instances where I have suppressed or hidden my true feelings? What were the circumstances surrounding these experiences?

4. What emotions do I find most difficult to express, and why do I think this is the case?

5. How do I believe embracing emotional vulnerability could positively impact my relationships, my work life, and my overall well-being?

Take your time with these reflections and allow yourself to be honest and introspective. By gaining a deeper understanding of your own experiences with emotional suppression, you can begin to unravel the hidden struggles that may be holding you back.

Journaling

Journaling can be a powerful tool for exploring your emotions in a private and introspective setting. Use the following prompts to guide your journaling practice:

1. Describe a recent situation where you felt pressure to hide or suppress your emotions. How did you respond in that moment, and how did it make you feel?

2. Reflect on a time when you allowed yourself to be vulnerable with someone else. What was the outcome of that experience, and how did it impact your relationship?

3. Write about a particular emotion that you find challenging to express. What are the underlying reasons behind your difficulty expressing this emotion?

4. Imagine a world where vulnerability is celebrated as strength. How would your life be different in this ideal scenario, and what steps can you take to move closer to this reality?

5. Consider the role of community support in embracing emotional vulnerability. How can you seek out supportive communities, both online and in-person, to share your experiences and find solidarity with others on a similar journey?

Commit to a regular journaling practice, whether it's daily, weekly, or whenever you feel the need to explore your emotions more deeply. Allow yourself the freedom to express your thoughts and feelings without judgment, knowing that your journal is a safe space for self-reflection and growth.

Building a Support System:

Surrounding yourself with supportive people who value vulnerability is crucial. Here's how to find your tribe:

1. Seek Out Like-Minded Individuals: Look for online communities or support groups specifically focused on men's emotional well-being. Connecting with others who understand your struggles can be incredibly empowering.

2. Talk to a Therapist: A therapist can provide a safe space to explore your emotions and develop healthy coping mechanisms for emotional expression.

3. Open Up to Close Friends: Identify a trusted friend or family member whom you feel comfortable opening up to emotionally. Sharing your vulnerabilities can strengthen your bond and foster deeper connections.

Remember that you are not alone in your journey towards embracing emotional vulnerability. By actively engaging with supportive communities and seeking professional guidance when needed, you can cultivate greater self-awareness, resilience, and authenticity in your life

Key Takeaways

- Acknowledging the hidden struggle with emotional expression is the first step towards embracing vulnerability.

- Societal expectations and internal conflicts can significantly impact how men express their emotions

- Vulnerability is power: It takes courage to open up, but it strengthens relationships and fosters deeper connections

- Societal expectations and internal conflicts can significantly impact how men express their emotions.

- Recognizing the psychological impact of emotional suppression is crucial for overall well-being.

- Build your support system, and find communities or individuals who value vulnerability and authenticity.

- Reflection matters. Explore your experiences and identify what influences your emotional expression.

Now that you understand the hidden struggles and conflicts that are a result of the societal expectations of the vulnerable man, it's time to take deliberate action.

Reflect on past experiences, find supportive connections, and challenge the fear of vulnerability. Dive deeper into the next chapter. and discover how embracing your emotions can transform your life.

Chapter 2: The Power of Vulnerability

Vulnerability means being open to attack or harm. It can be physical or emotional. It's the willingness to expose our innermost feelings, fears, and insecurities. Allowing vulnerability creates space for genuine connections, empathy, and growth. Acknowledging vulnerability isn't a weakness. It's a courageous step towards understanding ourselves and others. Vulnerabilities invite compassion. It fosters resilience. Share your struggles with a friend. Admit limitations. Remember, it's okay to be vulnerable—it's where our strength lies.

Vulnerability fosters authentic connections, deep empathy, and personal growth. Individuals demonstrate courage by sharing their true selves. Genuine relationships are built on trust and understanding through embracing vulnerability. Vulnerability opens the door to healing, as it encourages honesty and emotional expression. It dismantles barriers to intimacy, fostering a sense of belonging and acceptance. Through vulnerability, individuals cultivate resilience and self-awareness, discovering strength in their authenticity. Moments of vulnerability lead to profound transformation. This results in greater empathy, connection, and a more meaningful life.

This chapter explores vulnerability's transformative power. Vulnerability is a courageous act. It fosters authentic connections and emotional intelligence. You will learn how to express emotions effectively. You will also learn how to create space for vulnerability in relationships. You will understand the positive impact of vulnerability. This will inspire you to embrace your authentic self. There is also an action plan to incorporate vulnerability into your life. This plan will empower you and showcase vulnerability's transformative power.

Redefining Vulnerability

Have you ever held back from expressing a genuine emotion because you worried it would be perceived as a weakness? It could have been sadness after a breakup, anxiety before a presentation, or fear during a conversation. Society often forces us to believe that showing emotions makes us seem weak. Emotions beyond happiness or confidence are particularly discouraged. But vulnerability wasn't a weakness but a hidden strength.

Strength in Vulnerability

The truth is that embracing vulnerability takes courage. It requires the strength to shed the masks we wear and expose our authentic selves, flaws and all. Consider the experience of public speaking. Stepping onto a stage and sharing your ideas in front of a crowd requires a certain level of confidence. Have you seen a speaker pause in their presentation to share a personal story or moment of vulnerability? Perhaps they confessed to feeling nervous or acknowledged a past struggle related to the topic. These moments of vulnerability can be incredibly powerful. They connect the speaker to the audience on a deeper level, fostering a sense of authenticity and genuineness that resonates far more than a perfectly scripted presentation.

Researchers at the University of Houston found that leaders who show vulnerability are more trustworthy and effective with their teams. The study suggests that vulnerability fosters a sense of connection and psychological safety within a group, ultimately leading to better collaboration and performance. So, the next time you feel a surge of vulnerability rising, don't push it down. Acknowledge it as a sign of your strength and courage to be authentic, even when it feels uncomfortable.

Research by Brené Brown, a leading expert on vulnerability, highlights the connection between vulnerability and courage. Her studies show that people viewed as more confident and authentic embrace their full range of emotions. They tend to have stronger relationships and are better at navigating life's challenges.

Let's face it, life isn't always sunshine and rainbows. We all experience sadness, anger, fear, and disappointment. Suppressing these emotions isn't healthy.

Courageous Transparency

Vulnerability isn't just about expressing negative emotions; it's about being genuine in all aspects of your life. Consider a situation where you're forced to work with someone you don't particularly like. The easy route might be to put on a fake smile and pretend everything is fine. But what if you were vulnerable, expressing your discomfort respectfully?

This act of transparency could open the door to a more honest and productive working relationship. It shows that you're a real person with genuine feelings, not just a robot programmed to get the job done. This authenticity fosters trust and respect, creating a more positive work environment for everyone.

Vulnerability is courageous transparency. It means showing up authentically, flaws and all. When we embrace vulnerability, we invite others to do the same. Authentic relationships are built on honesty and openness, and vulnerability is the key that unlocks the door to genuine connections. It's through vulnerability that we cultivate trust and understanding, fostering deeper, more meaningful relationships.

Practical Strategies for Vulnerability

We've established that vulnerability is a strength, not a weakness. But how do you translate that knowledge into action? How do you move from hiding your emotions to expressing them healthily and authentically? This section will explore practical strategies to bridge the gap between theory and practice, fostering emotional intelligence, open communication, and a mindful approach to vulnerability.

1. Emotional Intelligence: Recognizing and Expressing Your Feelings

The first step towards vulnerability is understanding your own emotions. This might sound cliche, but many of us go through life on autopilot, disconnected from our internal world.

Emotional intelligence (EQ) is the ability to recognize, understand, and manage your own emotions, as well as those of others.

Think about a time you felt overwhelmed or angry. Were you able to identify the source of your emotions? Did you healthily express them? Developing your EQ can help you answer these questions.

Here are some practical strategies to enhance your emotional intelligence:

- Mindfulness Meditation: Mindfulness practices, like meditation, help you become more aware of your thoughts and emotions without judgment. Taking a few minutes each day to simply focus on your breath and observe your emotions can be a powerful tool for self-awareness.

- Journaling: Journaling is another excellent way to explore your emotions. Writing down your thoughts and feelings can help you identify patterns and triggers, and gain a deeper understanding of your inner world.

- Identifying Body Cues: Our bodies often communicate our emotions before our minds catch up. Learn to recognize physical signs of anxiety, anger, or sadness - a racing heart, clenched fists, or a tightness in your chest. This awareness can help you identify your emotions at the moment and choose healthy ways to express them.

2. Open Communication Skills: Creating Space for Vulnerability

Once you understand your emotions, it's time to express them effectively. Here's where open communication skills come into play. Open communication involves honest and respectful dialogue, where both partners feel safe expressing their feelings.

Here are some key communication techniques to foster vulnerability:

- Active Listening: Pay close attention to what the other person is saying, both verbally and nonverbally. Avoid interrupting and make eye contact to show you're engaged.

- "I" Statements: Instead of blaming or accusing language, use "I" statements to express your emotions. For example, instead of saying, "You always make me feel bad," try, "I feel hurt when you..." This approach focuses on your feelings and reduces defensiveness toward the other person.

- Validate Their Feelings: Acknowledge the other person's emotions and let them know their feelings are valid. This creates a safe space for them to express themselves openly.

Psychological Benefits of Vulnerability

Remember the last time you confided in a friend about a deep worry or a personal setback? Did sharing that burden lift a weight off your shoulders? Or perhaps, have you ever witnessed someone open up about their struggles and, in turn, felt a surge of connection and understanding? These are just a few of the remarkable benefits of vulnerability – reduced stress and increased empathy.

Vulnerability as a Stress-Buster

Research published in the journal Psychosomatic Medicine reveals a fascinating connection between vulnerability and stress reduction. The study found that individuals who practiced vulnerability by expressing their emotions openly experienced lower levels of stress hormones like cortisol.

Here's why vulnerability helps you manage stress:

- Release and Regulation: Bottling up emotions is like stuffing a balloon; eventually, the pressure builds, and it pops. Vulnerability allows you to release those pent-up emotions healthily. By expressing your feelings, you can begin to process and regulate them, leading to a calmer and more centered state of mind.

- Social Support System: When you open up to a trusted friend or family member, you create an opportunity for support. Sharing your struggles allows them to offer empathy, understanding, and practical help. This social support system can be a powerful buffer against stress.

- Self-Compassion: Vulnerability can also foster self-compassion. By acknowledging your emotions and accepting yourself as a human being with flaws and vulnerabilities, you can develop a kinder and more understanding relationship with yourself. This self-compassion reduces stress and promotes emotional well-being.

The Empathy Advantage

Vulnerability isn't just good for you; it's good for your relationships, and one of the most beautiful aspects of vulnerability is its ability to foster empathy. Empathy is the ability to understand and share the feelings of others. When you open up about your struggles, you create a space for others to do the same. This shared vulnerability strengthens connections and builds a sense of "we're all in this together."

A study published in the Journal of Personality and Social Psychology explored the link between vulnerability and empathy. The study found that individuals who disclosed personal information about themselves were perceived as more empathetic and trustworthy by others.

Here's how vulnerability strengthens relationships through empathy:

- Deeper Connections: Vulnerability allows you to connect with others on a deeper level. By sharing your authentic self, you create a sense of intimacy and trust that fosters stronger bonds.

- Improved Communication: Open communication is crucial for healthy relationships. When you're vulnerable with someone, you're more likely to communicate your needs and feelings effectively. This leads to less conflict and a deeper sense of understanding between partners.

- Building Trust: Vulnerability requires trust. When you open up to someone, you're essentially placing your trust in them. This act of trust strengthens the bond and creates a safe space for both partners to be vulnerable.

Vulnerability in the Workplace

The benefits of vulnerability extend beyond personal relationships. Research suggests that vulnerability can also have a positive impact on professional relationships. A study published in the Harvard Business Review found that leaders who displayed vulnerability by admitting mistakes and expressing emotions were perceived as more authentic and relatable by their employees. This, in turn, led to increased employee engagement and productivity.

The Ripple Effect of Vulnerability

The benefits of vulnerability extend far beyond the individual. When you embrace vulnerability and build strong, empathetic relationships, you create a ripple effect. These positive connections foster a more supportive and compassionate environment, impacting everyone around you.

Imagine a workplace where employees feel comfortable expressing their concerns and challenges. This vulnerability can lead to a more collaborative and productive environment. Or consider a community where individuals openly share their struggles. This openness can foster a sense of belonging and support, leading to a stronger and more resilient community.

By embracing vulnerability, you not only reduce your stress and increase your empathy, but you also contribute to a more positive and connected world.

Action Plan for Embracing Emotional Vulnerabilities

The world often praises strength and resilience but shames vulnerability. It's hard to be open and authentic.

This section provides an action plan to guide you in embracing vulnerability. Reflect on past experiences. Practice transparent communication. Engage in a mindful vulnerability challenge. Journal for reflection. Unlock vulnerability's potential. Build a fulfilling life.

Reflecting on Vulnerability's Strength

Let's take a moment for some introspection. Think back to a time in your life when you were vulnerable. Perhaps you opened up to a friend about a personal struggle, shared a hidden fear with a loved one, or expressed gratitude to someone who made a difference in your life.

- How did your vulnerability impact the outcome of the situation?

- Did it lead to a deeper connection with the other person?

- Did you experience a sense of relief or catharsis from expressing your true emotions?

Jot down your reflections in a journal or discuss them with a trusted friend. By reflecting on past experiences of vulnerability, you can reframe it as a strength, something that enhances your relationships and enriches your life. This awareness can empower you to embrace vulnerability with greater confidence in the future.

The Power of Transparent Communication

Effective communication is the cornerstone of healthy relationships. Vulnerability plays a crucial role in achieving transparent communication. But how do you translate your emotions into clear and honest communication?

Transparent communication takes practice. Start by incorporating these techniques into small conversations with friends and family. The more you practice, the easier it becomes to express your emotions openly and honestly.

Mindful Vulnerability Challenge

Are you ready to take your vulnerability to the next level? Here's a week-long challenge to help you integrate vulnerability into different aspects of your life:

- **Day 1:** Compliment a Stranger: Step outside your comfort zone and compliment someone you don't know well. This simple act of vulnerability can brighten their day and spark a positive interaction.

- **Day 2:** Share a Concern with a Loved One: Do you have a concern regarding a relationship with a friend or family member? Schedule some time to have a heart-to-heart conversation. Express your feelings honestly and listen openly to their perspective.

- **Day 3:** Write a Heartfelt Letter: Take some time to write a letter expressing gratitude or appreciation to someone who has made a significant impact on your life. The act of expressing your emotions in writing can be a powerful form of vulnerability.

- **Day 4:** Practice Active Listening with Empathy: During a conversation with a friend or colleague, actively listen to their emotions. Show empathy by validating their feelings and offering support if needed.

- **Day 5:** Express a Fear: Have you been holding onto a secret fear? Share this fear with a trusted friend or therapist. Expressing your vulnerabilities can be liberating and help you gain a new perspective.

- **Day 6:** Ask for Help: We all need help sometimes. Don't be afraid to ask for assistance when you need it. Doing so demonstrates vulnerability and allows others to offer support.

- **Day 7:** Journal your Reflections: Take some time to reflect on your week-long vulnerability challenge. Did you notice any changes in your relationships or emotional well-being? Journaling these reflections will help you understand the impact of vulnerability in your life.

This challenge is designed to empower you to step outside your comfort zone and engage in intentional vulnerability. Remember, vulnerability is not a one-time event; it's an ongoing process. The more you practice, the more comfortable you'll become with expressing your true emotions.

Journaling for Deeper Insights

Journaling is a powerful tool for self-discovery and reflection. Throughout this week, take some time after each vulnerability challenge to document your experiences in your journal. Here are some prompts to guide your reflections:

- How did expressing vulnerability make you feel (anxious, relieved, or empowered)?

- Did you notice any changes in your relationships with others?

- Did you experience any unexpected outcomes from your vulnerability?

- What did you learn about yourself from this experience?

By journaling your reflections, you can gain valuable insights into the impact of vulnerability on your emotional well-being, relationships, and overall sense of self.

Key Takeaways

- Strength in Vulnerability: Embracing your full range of emotions is a courageous act, not a weakness.

- Transparency Builds Bridges: Vulnerability fosters deeper connections by creating a space for courageous transparency.

- Emotional Intelligence Matters: Understanding your emotions is the first step towards expressing them effectively.

- Open Communication is Key: Effective communication is the cornerstone of healthy relationships, and vulnerability plays a crucial role in achieving transparent communication

- Mindfulness for Clarity: Mindfulness practices can help you manage strong emotions and express them clearly.

- Vulnerability Reduces Stress: Bottling up emotions can lead to stress; expressing them can be liberating.

- Deeper Connections: Vulnerability allows you to connect with others on a deeper, more meaningful level.

- Personal Growth: Expressing your true self opens doors for personal growth and a more fulfilling life.

Are you ready to embrace your vulnerability? This week, put the learnings into action with our mindful vulnerability challenge. In the next chapter, we'll explore redefining male empathy in a cultural context, and we'll also unlock strategies for a more emotionally authentic future.

Chapter 3: Emotional Vulnerability in Relationships

Imagine a world where expressing your true feelings isn't seen as a weakness but as a sign of strength. A world where men feel comfortable sharing their hopes, fears, and vulnerabilities with their partners, fostering deeper connections and a more fulfilling love life. This world is within reach, but it requires a shift in perspective—a redefinition of male empathy in our cultural context. Men should feel comfortable sharing their hopes, fears, and vulnerabilities.

Throughout history, societal expectations have often discouraged men from expressing their emotions openly.

This chapter explores how expectations affect male empathy in close relationships. We'll explore how embracing vulnerability can strengthen the emotional connection, communication, and trust between partners. We'll also address the challenges men face in navigating vulnerability and provide practical strategies to foster a more emotionally authentic and fulfilling romantic life.

Understanding the Impact of Emotional Vulnerability

Enhanced Emotional Intimacy

Intimacy goes beyond physical closeness. It's about feeling truly seen, heard, and understood by your partner. Vulnerability—the act of expressing your true emotions, both positive and negative, creates a space for this deeper connection to flourish.

In a published journal about personality and social relationships. Researchers discovered that couples who shared feelings and experiences reported higher levels of intimacy. They also reported greater relationship satisfaction.

Here's how vulnerability fosters emotional intimacy:

1. Creating a Safe Space: When you open up about your vulnerabilities, you invite your partner to do the same. This reciprocal exchange brings about a sense of safety and trust. You're saying, "I trust you enough to show you my true self, imperfections and all." This creates a safe haven for open communication and emotional connection.

2. Strengthening Emotional Bonds: Sharing your vulnerabilities allows your partner to connect with you on a deeper level. Imagine confiding in your partner about a childhood trauma. Their empathy and understanding create a stronger emotional bond. They see beyond the surface, connecting with your inner

world. This then creates a sense of closeness and intimacy that transcends the superficial.

3. Validation and Acceptance: Vulnerability allows your partner to validate your emotions. A supportive partner acknowledges your feelings, letting you know you're not alone. Validation fosters a sense of acceptance and belonging, deepening the emotional connection between you.

Transforming Communication Dynamics

Communication is the lifeblood of any relationship. But sometimes, unspoken emotions and unspoken needs can create misunderstandings and distance. Vulnerability can be the key to unlocking more effective communication.

1. Honest Expression: Vulnerability allows you to express your feelings honestly without bottling them up or resorting to passive-aggressiveness. This creates a space for open and direct communication, reducing the chances of misunderstandings.

2. Conflict Resolution: When disagreements arise, vulnerability can help navigate them more constructively. Sharing how a situation makes you feel allows your partner to understand your perspective and respond with empathy.

3. Strengthened Problem-Solving: By openly communicating your needs and concerns, you and your partner can work together to find solutions to problems. This collaborative approach fosters a sense of teamwork and strengthens your relationship.

Building a Foundation of Trust

Trust is the cornerstone of any healthy relationship. Vulnerability plays a critical role in building and strengthening this foundation.

1. Emotional Availability: When you open yourself up emotionally, you demonstrate trust in your partner. This creates a sense of security and allows the relationship to flourish. When you share a deeply personal secret with your partner, their supportive response and willingness to hold this information safely reinforce trust.

2. Creating a Sense of Security: Vulnerability fosters a sense of security in a relationship. By sharing your vulnerabilities, you make yourself open to your partner's support. This creates a sense of mutual reliance and strengthens the feeling of being in a safe and supportive space.

3. Greater Vulnerability, Greater Trust: The cycle of vulnerability and trust is reciprocal. The more you share your true self, the more trust you build. This increased trust, in turn, allows you to be even more vulnerable, creating a positive feedback loop that deepens your connection with your partner.

Challenges in Navigating Intimate Connections

We've explored how vulnerability can spice up deeper connections in romantic relationships. But let's be honest, embracing vulnerability isn't always sunshine and rainbows. There are challenges to navigate, and it's important to acknowledge these hurdles before taking the plunge.

Fear of Rejection

The fear of rejection is perhaps the biggest obstacle to vulnerability. Sharing your true feelings leaves you exposed, and the possibility of your partner not reciprocating can be daunting. This fear stems from a fundamental human need for connection and belonging. Rejection, in this context, feels like a threat to those core needs.

Here's how to overcome the fear of rejection and embrace vulnerability:

- Reframing Rejection: Rejection doesn't have to be a permanent roadblock. Sometimes, it's simply a sign of incompatibility. View rejection as an opportunity for growth and a chance to find a partner who truly appreciates your vulnerability.

- Start Small: You don't have to pour your heart out on the first date. Start by sharing small vulnerabilities, gradually building your comfort level. This allows your partner to reciprocate your openness, fostering a sense of emotional safety.

- Focus on the Potential Gains: Instead of dwelling on the potential for rejection, focus on the potential rewards of vulnerability. A deeper connection, stronger trust, and a more fulfilling relationship are all within reach.

- Celebrate Vulnerability Victories: Acknowledge and celebrate your progress. Each time you express a vulnerability, no matter how small, it's a victory over your fear.

Vulnerability Imbalance

Imagine you're excitedly sharing your hopes and dreams with your partner, but their response is muted or dismissive. This imbalance in vulnerability can create tension and strain in a relationship.

Here's why:

- Feeling Unheard and Unsupported: The partner who is more open emotionally may feel unheard or unsupported if their vulnerability isn't reciprocated. This can lead to feelings of frustration and resentment.

- Pressure to Conform: The less vulnerable partner may feel pressured to conform to their partner's level of emotional expression. This can lead to inauthenticity and a sense of suffocation in the relationship.

- The Blame Game: When vulnerability isn't balanced, blame can easily creep in. The more vulnerable partner may blame the other for not being open enough, creating a vicious cycle of negativity.

Strategies for Achieving Balanced Vulnerability

1. Open Communication is Key: Talk to your partner about your desired level of vulnerability in the relationship. Communicate your needs and listen openly to theirs.

2. Respect Individual Differences: People have different comfort levels with vulnerability. Respect your partner's pace and encourage them to gradually step outside their comfort zone.

3. Focus on Mutual Growth: Frame vulnerability as a journey you're taking together. Celebrate each other's progress and create a safe space for both partners to explore their emotional landscapes.

4. Lead by Example: If you want your partner to be more vulnerable, be a role model.

Express your own vulnerabilities authentically and show them the emotional rewards of openness.

By addressing these challenges and building an environment of mutual respect and understanding, you can navigate the vulnerability tightrope and create a more fulfilling and connected relationship.

Real-Life Couples: Vulnerability as a Bridge to Deeper Connection

One Sunday evening, I decided to organize a brunch with my close friends, all married couples. The brunch's main purpose was for each couple to share their relationship journeys. They discussed the challenges they faced and how they navigated them.

We discussed emotional vulnerability's impact on relationships. Men's struggle to open up was a key focus.

Here are some of their stories:

1. Jessica & Ethan: From Frustration to Forgiveness

Jessica, a successful lawyer, found herself constantly frustrated by Ethan's emotionless demeanor. After months of bottling up her feelings, she decided to have an honest conversation. Tears streamed down her face as she confessed feeling unheard and emotionally distant. Ethan, initially taken aback, listened intently without interrupting. He then surprised her by sharing his struggles—a fear of failure he'd never spoken of before. This shared vulnerability opened a floodgate of emotions. They spent hours talking, offering comfort and understanding. The next morning, they woke up feeling closer than ever before. The experience strengthened their bond. It taught them the importance of creating a safe space for emotional expression.

2. David & Alex: Career Dreams and Relationship Realities

David, an aspiring writer, felt increasingly burdened by the financial pressure of supporting their family. He harbored a secret dream of pursuing his writing full-time, but fear of Alex's disapproval kept him silent. One evening, after a particularly stressful day, he decided to take a chance. He confessed his anxieties and his long-held dream. Alex, instead of being dismissive, surprised him with her unwavering support. She acknowledged his sacrifices and expressed her belief in his talent. This shared vulnerability allowed them to have a difficult but honest conversation about their finances and priorities. Together, they came up with a plan to support David's writing dream while ensuring their family's stability.

3. Sarah & Michael: Overcoming Past Hurts

Sarah, recently out of a long-term relationship, found it difficult to trust Michael fully. Memories of past betrayals left her guarded and hesitant to open up emotionally. One night, after a fight, Michael took a different approach. Instead of getting defensive, he shared his vulnerabilities about past relationship insecurities. This unexpected move disarmed Sarah. She began to share her fears, and they spent the night talking openly and honestly. This shared vulnerability created a space for healing and forgiveness. Sarah started to trust Michael more deeply, and their relationship blossomed.

These real-life stories illustrate the transformative power of shared vulnerability. When both partners are willing to open up emotionally, it creates a ripple effect:

- Deeper Understanding: Sharing your vulnerabilities allows your partner to see the world from your perspective. This fosters empathy and a deeper understanding of your emotional landscape.

- Strengthened Trust: Reciprocal vulnerability is a cornerstone of trust. By opening yourself up emotionally, you demonstrate your trust in your partner's ability to handle your true feelings. This trust, in turn, strengthens the foundation of your relationship.

- Greater Intimacy: Shared vulnerability allows you to connect with your partner on a deeper and more meaningful level. You create a safe space for emotional intimacy where both partners feel seen, heard, and understood.

A healthy relationship thrives on reciprocity. While one partner initiating vulnerability is a positive step, it's crucial to encourage a two-way flow of emotions.

Here's why reciprocity matters:

- Balanced Connection: A relationship where only one partner expresses vulnerabilities becomes lopsided and unsustainable. Reciprocity creates a balanced dynamic where both partners feel comfortable sharing their emotions.

- Mutual Respect and Support: When both partners are vulnerable, it demonstrates a sense of mutual respect and support. You're essentially saying, "I trust you enough to share my vulnerabilities, and I'm here for yours too."

- Emotional Growth Together: The journey of vulnerability is a shared experience. By encouraging each other to step outside your comfort zones, you can both grow emotionally and create a more fulfilling relationship.

Remember, reciprocity doesn't mean forcing your partner to share at your pace. It's about creating a safe and supportive environment where they feel comfortable expressing their vulnerabilities in their own time.

By embracing shared vulnerability, you can build a bridge of trust, understanding, and intimacy, creating a more fulfilling and connected relationship.

Level Up with This Vulnerability Game: Creative Exercises for Couples

We've covered the foundational aspects of vulnerability in relationships. Now, let's dive into some engaging exercises that go beyond the typical conversation starters. These activities are designed to spark deeper connections and encourage vulnerability in a fun and creative way:

1. **The "36 Questions" Exercise:** Developed by psychologist Arthur Aron, this set of 36 increasingly personal questions is designed to foster intimacy and connection. Take turns asking each other the questions, offering honest and open answers.
Download here:
https://amorebeautifulquestion.com/wp-content/uploads/2024/02/Arthur-Arons-36-questions-2.pdf

2. **The "Dear Younger You" Letter:** This exercise takes inspiration from childhood memories. Grab a pen and paper and write a letter to your younger self, addressing any insecurities or challenges you faced. Then, share this letter with your partner. This act of vulnerability allows you to explore your emotional landscape and fosters empathy from your partner.

3. **The "Vulnerability Jar":** Turn vulnerability into a playful challenge. Take a jar and decorate it together. Throughout the week, write down moments where you felt vulnerable, either positive or negative (e.g., "I opened up about my anxieties about work"). At the end of the week, pick a random note from the jar and discuss the experience with your partner. his injects an element of surprise and encourages open communication.

4. **The "Strength Through Vulnerability" Collage:** This activity is a powerful visual representation of your emotional journey. Create a collage together using magazine clippings, photos, or drawings. Include images that represent moments of vulnerability in your relationship, alongside images that

symbolize the strength and growth that emerged from those experiences. Discuss the collage together, reflecting on your shared journey of vulnerability.

5. The "Non-Verbal Vulnerability Challenge": Sometimes, words can be limiting. Dedicate an evening to expressing vulnerabilities through non-verbal cues. This could involve acting out a scenario where you felt vulnerable, creating a piece of art that reflects your emotions, or writing a short poem for each other. This exercise encourages emotional expression beyond words and can lead to a deeper understanding.

6. The "Gratitude Walk": Combine gratitude with vulnerability for a powerful bonding experience. Take a walk together in nature and take turns expressing things you appreciate about each other, your relationship, or yourselves. This fosters a sense of positivity and creates a space for deeper emotional connection.

Remember, the key is to find what works best for you as a couple. Embrace creativity, have fun with these exercises, and most importantly, celebrate each other's vulnerabilities. By stepping outside your comfort zones together, you'll strengthen your bond and create a more fulfilling relationship.

Key Takeaways

- Vulnerability fosters deeper emotional intimacy by creating a safe space for genuine connection.

- Open communication thrives on vulnerability, leading to more honest and productive conversations.

- Vulnerability strengthens trust by demonstrating your faith in your partner's ability to handle your emotions.

- Fear of rejection and vulnerability imbalances can hinder emotional connection – address these challenges openly.

- Shared vulnerability, a two-way street, fosters deeper understanding, strengthens trust, and creates a more fulfilling relationship.

- Utilize exercises like the "36 Questions" to build a safe space for vulnerability.

- Spice things up with creative exercises like the "Dear Younger You Letter" or the "Vulnerability Jar" to explore vulnerability playfully.

- Non-verbal exercises like creating art or poems together can encourage deeper emotional expression.

- Gratitude walks promote positivity and create a space for deeper emotional connection in your relationship.

By implementing these strategies, you'll enhance intimacy and foster a healthier relationship. Ready to unlock the full potential of emotions? Dive into the next chapter for insights on mastering emotional expression. The chapter offers actionable advice for your relationship

Chapter 4: The Language of Emotions

Have you ever felt overwhelmed by emotions but couldn't express them clearly? Perhaps you ended up saying something you didn't mean, or the other person completely misinterpreted your feelings. This is where mastering the language of emotions becomes crucial. Just like any other language, emotions have their own vocabulary and communication styles.

Trying to have a complex conversation in a foreign language with only a few words makes it hard to convey the correct message. That's what it's like when your emotional vocabulary is limited. Develop your emotional fluency. This helps you understand your feelings and communicate effectively in relationships. You'll be able to move beyond simple labels like "happy" or "sad" and express a wider range of emotions with precision. This new fluency will help you build better connections. It will also help you handle disagreements well. You can create a more satisfying emotional landscape in every part of your life.

With this chapter, you will be able to understand and express your emotions effectively. You will see the importance of emotional vocabulary, explore diverse communication styles, and offer practical exercises to enhance your emotional expression. Get ready to unlock the transformative power of emotional intelligence and build stronger, more meaningful connections.

Understanding the Language of Emotions

Emotions are the vibrant hues that paint the canvas of our lives. Emotions shape experiences, influence decisions, and connect people. Yet, how often do we pause to truly understand how our feelings work?

Imagine emotions as words—each one carrying a distinct shade, texture, and resonance. A broad emotional vocabulary lets us express subtle feelings. It's like having a broader palette to paint with, allowing us to create emotional masterpieces.

Why Does Emotional Vocabulary Matter?

- Precision in Expression: When we label an emotion, we give it form and substance. Instead of merely feeling "off," we can say, "I'm feeling anxious." This specificity helps us communicate more effectively with others and ourselves.

- Self-Awareness: Emotional literacy—the ability to recognize, described, and understand feelings—enhances self-awareness. It's like turning on a light in the dimly lit corridors of our psyche. We become attuned to the subtle shifts within us.

- Emotional Regulation: Imagine having a toolbox filled with tools for different tasks. Emotional vocabulary is one such tool. When we can describe our emotions, we have control over them. We can soothe anxiety, channel anger constructively, and savor joy consciously.

Emotional Vocabulary and Well-Being: The Science Behind It

A study in the Journal of Personality and Social Psychology shows that people with a broad emotional vocabulary have higher emotional well-being.

Here's what they discovered:

1. Negative Emotion Vocabulary and Distress:

People who use a wider variety of negative emotional words tend to display signs of lower well-being.

These signs include references to illness, loneliness, and other signs of psychological distress.

Individuals with an extensive negative emotion vocabulary experience more depression and neuroticism. They also have worse physical health.

2. Positive Emotion Vocabulary and Flourishing:

People who use positive emotional words show signs of well-being.

These signs include references to leisure activities, achievements, and belonging to a group.

People with a broad positive emotion vocabulary tend to have higher conscientiousness, extraversion, and agreeableness.

They also enjoy better overall health and experience lower rates of depression and neuroticism.

Building Your Emotional Vocabulary

Ready to embark on your journey to emotional fluency? Here are some practical tips to expand your emotional vocabulary:

1. Pay attention to the subtle emotions you experience daily. Instead of labeling everything as "good" or "bad," try to identify the specific feeling. Are you feeling frustrated, anxious, or perhaps a sense of accomplishment?

2. Read Literature and Watch Films: Pay attention to how authors and filmmakers depict a range of emotions through their characters' words and actions. This can inspire you to expand your own emotional vocabulary.

Beyond Words: Exploring Expressive Communication Styles

Not everyone expresses emotions verbally. Some people are naturally more expressive through body language, facial expressions, or creative outlets. Recognizing your own communication style and that of those around you is key to effective emotional expression:

- The Verbal Expresser: These individuals readily express their emotions through words. They might initiate conversations about their feelings and readily share their thoughts and opinions.

- The Non-verbal Expresser: These people communicate emotions more through their body language, facial expressions, and tone of voice. Paying close attention to these nonverbal cues is crucial to understanding their feelings.

- The Creative Expresser: Some individuals find solace in expressing emotions through creative outlets like art, music, or writing. These activities can be powerful tools for emotional release and self-exploration.

Understanding Your Communication Style

Reflect on how you typically express your emotions. Do you find yourself talking things through, or do you withdraw and process internally? Perhaps you gravitate towards creative expression to navigate complex emotions. Understanding your natural style helps you choose communication methods that resonate with you. You can effectively convey your feelings to others.

Adapting Your Communication

While knowing your own style is important, effective communication often involves adapting to the communication styles of others. Here are some tips:

- Observe Nonverbal Cues: Pay attention to body language, facial expressions, and tone of voice to understand the emotional undercurrents of a conversation.

- Ask Clarifying Questions: If you're unsure about someone's emotions, don't hesitate to ask clarifying questions in a gentle and respectful manner.

- Embrace Different Forms of Expression: Recognize that others might express emotions differently than you do. Be open to understanding their unique communication style.

Expand your emotional vocabulary and recognize diverse communication styles. This will help you navigate human connections effectively. In the next section, we'll explore practical exercises to further enhance your emotional expression.

Communication Techniques for Authentic Expression

Effective emotional expression isn't just about conveying your own feelings; it's also about creating a space where others feel heard and understood. This two-way street of communication is crucial for building strong and healthy relationships.

This section covers two key techniques: active listening and "I" statements. They help you navigate conversations with more emotional intelligence.

Active Listening: The Art of Truly Hearing

Have you ever felt like you're talking to a brick wall during a conversation? Perhaps your partner seems distracted, or a friend interrupts you mid-sentence. These experiences highlight the importance of active listening, a skill that goes beyond simply hearing someone's words.

Active listening involves paying full attention to the speaker, both verbally and nonverbally. It's about creating a safe space where the other person feels comfortable expressing themselves openly and honestly. Research from the University of California, Los Angeles, suggests that active listening can foster empathy, trust, and positive communication outcomes.

Essential Elements of Active Listening:

- Give Your Full Attention: Put away distractions like your phone and make eye contact with the speaker. This conveys your interest and encourages them to continue sharing.

- Listen Verbally and Nonverbally: Pay attention to both the words being spoken and the underlying emotions conveyed through body language, facial expressions, and tone of voice.

- Use Verbal Cues: Acknowledge the speaker with nonverbal cues like head nods or brief interjections like "mm-hmm" to show you're engaged.

- Ask Clarifying Questions: Don't be afraid to ask questions to ensure you understand their perspective. Phrase your questions in a way that encourages elaboration, not judgment.

- Summarize and Reflect: Periodically summarize what you've heard to demonstrate your understanding and encourage further elaboration.

By actively listening, you create a safe space for emotional expression and show genuine care for the other person's feelings.

The Power of "I" Statements: Owning Your Emotions

Have you ever tried expressing your feelings, only to have the conversation escalate into a blame game? This is where "I" statements come in. "I" statements are a powerful tool for expressing your emotions in a way that takes ownership without placing blame on the other person.

Here's the difference:

- "You" Statement: "You always make me feel bad when you..." (This is accusatory and can shut down communication)

- "I" Statement: "I feel hurt when you..." (This focuses on your feelings and opens the door for a constructive conversation)

Benefits of Using "I" Statements:

- Promotes Self-Awareness: "I" statements encourage you to identify and acknowledge your own emotions before expressing them to others.

- Reduces Blame: By focusing on your feelings, you avoid accusatory language that can trigger defensiveness in the other person.

- Encourages Open Communication: "I" statements create a space for the other person to understand your perspective and respond constructively.

Formulating Effective "I" Statements:

Crafting clear and concise "I" statements takes practice. Here's a simple formula:

I feel (emotion) when (describe the situation). Because (explain the impact of the situation)

"I" Statements in Practice:

Imagine you're feeling frustrated because your partner keeps leaving their dirty dishes in the sink. Here's how an "I" statement can help:

"I feel frustrated (emotion) when I see dirty dishes left in the sink (describe the situation). Because I feel like I'm always the one cleaning up (explain the impact)."

This approach focuses on your feelings and opens the door for a collaborative solution.

"I" statements promote personal responsibility and accountability in communication while fostering mutual respect and validation. They encourage a collaborative approach to problem-solving and conflict resolution, creating a supportive environment where both parties feel heard and valued.

Navigating Difficult Conversations

Life is full of disagreements, hurt feelings, and misunderstandings. Difficult conversations are inevitable, but they don't have to be destructive. The solution is not to avoid tough conversations. Instead, navigate them with emotional intelligence. This ensures a productive result.

Conflict Resolution Strategies

Conflict can be a catalyst for growth and positive change. Approaching with anger, blame, or defensiveness escalates issues and prevents resolution.

Here are some strategies to navigate difficult conversations with emotional intelligence:

1. Choose the Right Time and Place: Don't initiate a heated conversation when emotions are running high. Choose a calm moment when both parties are available for a focused discussion.

2. Set the Tone: By expressing your feelings and concerns in a way that avoids blame. This helps the other person feel heard and less likely to become defensive.

3. Listen: Pay close attention to both verbal and nonverbal cues. Acknowledge their perspective and ask clarifying questions to ensure understanding.

4. Focus on Problem-Solving, Not Blame: Shift the focus from who's right or wrong to finding a solution that works for everyone involved.

5. Be Willing to Compromise: Finding common ground is key to resolving conflict. Be open to different perspectives and be prepared to compromise to reach a mutually beneficial agreement.

The Power of Empathy

Empathy is the ability to understand and share the feelings of another person. During charged conversations, empathy is crucial for fostering understanding and building bridges.

University of California, Berkeley studies show empathy reduces negative emotions. Empathy also promotes cooperation in conflict resolution. Here are some tips to cultivate empathy in communication:

1. Listen Without Judgment: Set aside your own biases and truly try to understand the other person's perspective.

2. Validate Their Feelings: Acknowledge their emotions, even if you don't agree with them. Phrases like "It sounds like you're feeling..." can go a long way.

3. See Things from Their Perspective: Try to understand the situation from their point of view. What are their concerns? What might be driving their emotions?

Difficult conversations are an opportunity for growth and connection. Express your emotions effectively, employ conflict resolution strategies, and cultivate empathy. This way, you can navigate situations with more emotional intelligence, fostering stronger relationships.

Key Takeaways

- Unlocking Your Inner Voice: Mastering emotional expression empowers you to navigate your inner world with greater clarity and communicate your feelings authentically.

- Building Your Emotional Vocabulary: Expand your vocabulary beyond "happy" and "sad" to identify and express a wider range of emotions with precision.

- Express Yourself Beyond Words: Explore creative outlets like art, music, or writing to release and explore emotions in a unique way.

- Active Listening is Key: Pay close attention to both verbal and nonverbal cues to truly understand the emotions of others.

- "I" Statement: Utilize "I" statements to express your feelings without blame, fostering healthier communication.

- Navigating Conflict with Ease: Employ conflict resolution strategies and empathy to navigate difficult conversations productively.

- Understanding Leads to Connection: By actively listening and expressing yourself clearly, you can build stronger, more meaningful relationships.

- Problem-Solving, Not Blame Games: Focus on finding solutions that work for everyone involved during disagreements.

- Practice Makes Progress: The more you practice expressing your emotions effectively, the more comfortable and confident you'll become.

- Emotional Intelligence Empowers You: Developing your emotional intelligence equips you to face life's challenges with greater resilience and build a more fulfilling life.

Are you ready to take action? Choose one communication technique this week. Practice it daily. Perhaps you'll actively listen to a colleague with your full attention or use an "I" statement to express a concern to your manager. Remember, small changes can lead to big results in your emotional expression journey. The next chapter explores the unique challenges and opportunities of emotional expression at work, equipping you to navigate these situations with greater confidence and emotional intelligence.

Part 2: The Boardroom Balance - Applying Emotional Intelligence at Work

Chapter 5: The Workplace Dilemma

Is there always pressure to bottle up your emotions at work? You disagree with your colleague's approach during a tense negotiation. Expressing frustration could seem unprofessional at work. It might disrupt workplace harmony. Many men in professional settings often struggle with balancing authentic expression and fear of judgment. Navigating the unspoken rules at work is challenging. It underscores emotional expression challenges. This dilemma can cause stress, burnout, and strained relationships. It affects individual well-being and organizational dynamics. We will uncover strategies to navigate this challenge. We'll cultivate a work environment that values emotional authenticity.

This chapter delves into the complexities of emotional intelligence in the work sphere. We will discuss traditional work emotions, changes in emotional intelligence, and men's challenges. There are practical strategies and inspiring insights that empower you to navigate the workplace for career success.

The Emotional Landscape of the Workplace

For decades, professional settings have often prioritized logic and control. The unspoken rule? Keep your emotions in check. Passionate disagreement? Disruptive. This stoic ideal, however, comes at a cost. Let's see the traditional expectations surrounding emotional expression and explore the exciting shift towards emotional intelligence in modern workplaces.

Traditional Workplace Expectations

These expectations come from viewing the workplace as rational and objective. People viewed emotions as disruptive forces that clouded judgment and hindered productivity. This perspective created a culture favoring logic over emotions. Emotional expression was marginalized.

The consequences of this approach can be far-reaching. Stifling emotional expression can lead to:

- Miscommunication: Unexpressed emotions can fester, leading to misunderstandings and resentment between colleagues. Misinterpreted nonverbal cues can complicate communication.

- Hindered Collaboration: Innovation thrives in an environment where diverse perspectives are openly shared. When people fear judgment for expressing their true feelings, collaboration suffers, and the team misses out on valuable insights.

- Employee Disengagement: Feeling like you can't be your authentic self at work can be draining and lead to disengagement. Employees who suppress emotions may feel more stressed and less satisfied at work.

Modern workplaces increasingly recognize the value of emotional intelligence (EQ). EQ is the ability to understand, use, and manage emotions effectively. It helps individuals achieve their goals. In the workplace context, this translates to leaders and employees who can:

- Self-Awareness: Recognize their own emotions and how they impact their behavior.

- Emotional Regulation: Manage their emotions effectively, preventing them from clouding judgment.

- Motivation: Use their emotions to fuel motivation and drive results.

- Empathy: Understand and share the feelings of others, fostering stronger relationships.

- Social Skills: Build rapport, communicate effectively, and navigate conflict constructively.

The benefits of emotional intelligence in the workplace are undeniable. The Harvard Business Review studies show EQ is crucial for leadership success. EQ accounts for almost 90% of the top performers. Organizations with emotionally intelligent employees experience:

- Team members' open expression boosts collaboration and efficiency in problem-solving.

- Enhanced Innovation: A diverse range of perspectives, freely expressed, leads to more creative solutions and a competitive edge.

- Improved Conflict Resolution: EQ allows individuals to address disagreements constructively, focusing on solutions rather than blame.

- Positive Work Environment: Open communication and mutual respect foster a sense of trust and belonging, leading to higher employee engagement and satisfaction.

The traditional workplace may have valued stoicism, but the modern landscape demands a shift. Emotional intelligence is no longer a "soft skill" but a crucial asset for success. By building an environment where emotional expression is encouraged and emotional intelligence is valued, organizations can unlock the full potential of their workforce and create a thriving workplace culture.

Challenges Men Encounter in Emotional Expression at Work

For many men, expressing emotions beyond happiness or anger can carry a social stigma. Tears might be seen as weakness, frustration as unprofessional, and even excitement as childish. These stereotypes can be incredibly limiting, preventing men from expressing their full range of emotions and hindering genuine connection with colleagues.

The science behind emotions is clear: they are not signs of weakness but natural human responses. Studies by the American Psychological Association (APA) show that suppressing emotions can have negative consequences for our health.

This perception can lead to a self-silencing effect, hindering men from openly communicating their feelings and hindering their ability to connect with colleagues on a deeper level.

The consequences of these stereotypes can be significant:

1. Fear of Judgment: The fear of being perceived as weak or unprofessional can prevent men from voicing concerns, seeking help, or celebrating successes with genuine enthusiasm. This bottled-up energy can lead to increased stress and decreased motivation.

2. Missed Opportunities for Connection: Open communication is the cornerstone of strong relationships.

When men hold back their emotions, they may miss opportunities to build trust and rapport with colleagues, ultimately hindering collaboration and team dynamics.

3. Emotional Labor and Burnout: Constantly suppressing emotions can be emotionally draining. This emotional labor can lead to burnout, impacting a man's physical and mental well-being, as well as his work performance.

Navigating Hierarchical Structures

Hierarchical organizational structures can pose challenges for men when expressing vulnerability. In many workplaces, there's a perception that vulnerability is a sign of weakness, especially for those in leadership positions. Men may fear that showing vulnerability could undermine their authority or lead to being viewed as incompetent. This fear can inhibit honest communication and hinder meaningful connections with colleagues.

This dynamic can stifle open communication and hinder innovation.

Here's a closer look at the challenges:

- Power Dynamics: The traditional power imbalance in hierarchical structures can make men feel hesitant to challenge the status quo or express dissenting opinions, even if they have valuable insights to share.

- Fear of Undermining Authority: Openly expressing emotions, particularly frustration or doubt, might be seen as a sign of weakness or a lack of confidence in leadership.

- Limited Role Models: The lack of prominent male leaders who openly express a full range of emotions can create a sense of isolation for men navigating these challenges.

Despite the challenges, there are ways for men to navigate the emotional landscape of the workplace more effectively:

- Challenge the Narrative: Recognize and challenge the limiting stereotypes around masculinity. True strength lies in emotional intelligence, not stoicism.

- Find Your Voice: Practice expressing your emotions in a controlled and professional way. Start small, perhaps with a trusted colleague, and gradually build confidence in expressing yourself authentically.

- Seek Out Allies: Build a network of colleagues who value open communication and emotional intelligence. Having a support system can create a safe space for you to express yourself and navigate challenges.

Remember, leaders who can connect with their teams on an emotional level are seen as more inspiring and effective.

The Impact of Emotional Intelligence on Career Success

Emotional intelligence isn't just about managing your own emotions; it's about understanding and navigating the emotions of others. This skillset is essential for building strong relationships, a key factor in career advancement.

Here's how emotional intelligence empowers you on your professional journey:

- Stronger Networking: People are drawn to those who make them feel valued and understood. Emotional intelligence allows you to build rapport with colleagues and create a network of support that can open doors to new opportunities.

- Effective Communication: Clear and concise communication is crucial for success in any role. Emotional intelligence equips you to express your ideas persuasively, actively listen to others, and navigate difficult conversations with diplomacy.

- Teamwork and Collaboration: The modern workplace thrives on collaboration. Emotional intelligence allows you to work effectively within teams, manage conflict constructively, and inspire others to achieve common goals.

- Adaptability and Resilience: The ability to adapt to change and bounce back from setbacks is essential for long-term success. Emotional intelligence equips you to manage stress effectively, stay motivated, and persevere through challenges.

Leadership Lessons: The Power of Emotional Intelligence in Action

Perhaps the most significant impact of emotional intelligence lies in its power to shape effective leadership. Leaders with high EQ are not just competent; they inspire and motivate their teams.

Here are some key characteristics of emotionally intelligent leaders:

- Self-Awareness: Emotionally intelligent leaders understand their own strengths and weaknesses, allowing them to make informed decisions and lead with authenticity.

- Empathy: These leaders can put themselves in the shoes of their team members, fostering trust and creating a positive work environment.

- Motivation: They can inspire their teams to achieve their full potential by creating a shared vision and fostering a sense of purpose.

- Emotional Regulation: They can manage their emotions effectively, remaining calm and collected under pressure, which provides a sense of stability for their team.

Leading with Empathy: The Power of Emotional Intelligence in Leadership

In today's workplace, strong leadership is more than just barking orders. Effective leaders are those who can inspire, motivate, and unite their teams towards a common goal. This is where emotional intelligence takes center stage.

Here's how emotional intelligence fosters effective leadership:

- Building Trust and Psychological Safety: Leaders with high EQ create a safe space where team members feel comfortable sharing ideas, taking risks, and admitting mistakes. This fosters trust, innovation, and a sense of belonging within the team.

- Conflict Resolution: Teams inevitably face disagreements. Emotionally intelligent leaders can navigate conflict constructively, focusing on solutions rather than blame. This preserves morale and keeps the team moving forward.

- Motivating and Inspiring: Leaders with high EQ can understand the emotional needs of their team members and tailor their leadership style accordingly. They can inspire their teams to achieve great things.

A study by the Hay Group found that emotionally intelligent leaders are:

- 33% more effective at developing their people

- 27% more likely to be rated as high performers by their peers

- 17% more likely to have satisfied customers

These statistics highlight the undeniable impact of emotional intelligence on leadership effectiveness.

Strategies for Navigating the Workplace Dilemma

Emotional intelligence isn't a fixed trait; it's a skill that can be developed. Organizations that invest in emotional intelligence training programs reap significant benefits. These programs equip employees with the tools to:

- Identify Emotions: Recognize their own emotions and the emotions of others, both verbally and nonverbally.

- Understand Triggers: Pinpoint the situations or behaviors that trigger specific emotions.

- Manage Emotions Effectively: Develop healthy coping mechanisms to regulate their emotions in a constructive way.

- Empathize with Others: See things from another person's perspective and build stronger relationships.

- Communicate Effectively: Express their emotions clearly and professionally, fostering open communication.

The impact of emotional intelligence training is far-reaching. Organizations with emotionally intelligent employees experience:

- Increased Employee Engagement: Employees feel valued and invested in their work, leading to higher productivity and job satisfaction.

- Improved Conflict Resolution: EQ fosters constructive communication, allowing teams to address disagreements effectively.

- Enhanced Customer Service: Employees with strong emotional intelligence skills can build rapport with clients and provide exceptional service.

- Reduced Absenteeism and Turnover: A positive work environment, fostered by emotional intelligence, leads to a more stable and committed workforce.

Finding the Right Balance: Authenticity and Professionalism

Emotional intelligence isn't about becoming a walking emotional rollercoaster. It's about striking a balance between expressing yourself authentically and maintaining professionalism.

Here are some tips to achieve this balance:

- Choose Your Battles: Not every situation requires a full-blown emotional response. Learn to discern when it's appropriate to express your emotions and when it's best to take a breath and respond calmly.

- Express Yourself Constructively: Focus on communicating your feelings in a clear and professional manner. Instead of saying "I'm angry," try saying "I feel frustrated when..." and explain the reason behind your emotions.

- Consider the Context: The appropriate way to express your emotions will vary depending on the situation and the people you're interacting with. Use your judgment to determine the most professional way to communicate your feelings.

- Practice Makes Progress: Just like any other skill, emotional intelligence takes practice. Start by incorporating these strategies into your daily interactions, and gradually build your confidence.

- Seek Feedback: Ask trusted colleagues for feedback on your communication style. This can help you identify areas for improvement and ensure your emotional expression is being received as intended.

- Lead by Example: If you're in a leadership position, model emotionally intelligent behavior. By openly expressing your emotions appropriately, you can create a culture where emotional intelligence is valued and encouraged.

Key Takeaways

- Traditional workplaces discouraged emotional expression, hindering communication and collaboration.

- The tide is turning: Modern workplaces value emotional intelligence (EQ) for leadership and team success.

- Men face challenges expressing emotions: Stigmas, hierarchies, and communication styles can create barriers.

- EQ fuels career advancement: Effective communication, strong relationships, and emotional self-management are key.

- Leaders with high EQ are more effective: They build trust, inspire teams, and navigate conflict constructively.

- Emotional intelligence training equips you with skills: Identify emotions, manage them effectively, and build empathy.

- Balance authenticity and professionalism: Express your feelings clearly and constructively in a work-appropriate manner.

- Build a support network: Find colleagues who value open communication and emotional intelligence.

- Leaders who embrace EQ foster a positive work environment: Increased productivity, innovation, and employee satisfaction.

- Invest in your EQ: It's a crucial skill for navigating challenges, building a fulfilling career, and becoming a successful leader.

Now that you've gained insight into how to apply emotional intelligence at work, it's time to consider situations where emotions have impacted you at work. How could emotional intelligence have helped? Explore emotional intelligence training offered by your company or online platforms. Start small. Express your feelings clearly and professionally in a safe space with a trusted colleague. Seek out colleagues who value open communication and emotional intelligence.

Take the next step towards becoming an emotionally intelligent leader by proceeding to the next chapter. Explore practical strategies and insights to elevate your leadership skills and create a positive impact in your professional and personal lives.

Chapter 6: Emotional Leadership

Emotional leadership is a concept that emphasizes the importance of leaders being able to understand and manage their own emotions, as well as recognize and influence the emotions of those around them. It's based on the idea of emotional intelligence, which includes skills such as empathy, self-awareness, and the ability to manage relationships judiciously and empathetically.

Emotional leadership revolves around the ability of leaders to understand, regulate, and leverage emotions effectively. Leaders who excel in emotional intelligence can create a positive work environment, build strong teams, and navigate challenging situations with finesse.

This chapter dives deep into the transformative world of emotional leadership. We will discuss how EQ helps leaders. It shapes team dynamics positively. It fosters a culture of collaboration and trust. Inspiring profiles, practical strategies, and actionable steps will equip you to become an emotionally intelligent leader. This will help you ignite your team's potential.

Embark on a leadership journey where emotional intelligence is your most powerful tool.

Leadership styles have evolved dramatically over time. The stern, top-down commander is being replaced by a nuanced approach. This approach acknowledges the power of emotions. This is where emotional leadership takes center stage.

Emotional Leadership Defined: More Than Just Authority

Emotional leadership goes beyond simply giving orders and expecting results. Harness emotional intelligence (EQ) to create a positive work environment. This boosts productivity. Daniel Goleman, a pioneer in the field of EQ, defines emotional leadership as "the capacity of a leader to recognize their own emotions and those of their people and to use this awareness to motivate, empower, and develop their employees."

Emotional leadership involves building strong relationships with team members. Understanding their needs and motivations is crucial. Creating a safe space for them to express themselves is essential. This builds trust, belonging, and boosts engagement and performance.

The Benefits of Emotional Leadership: A Ripple Effect

The impact of emotional leadership extends far beyond the individual leader. Studies by the Center for Creative Leadership (CCL) show that emotionally intelligent leaders create teams with several key advantages:

- Increased Collaboration: Emotional leaders build trust by fostering psychological safety. Team members can share ideas openly and collaborate effectively toward a common goal.

- Enhanced Innovation: When team members feel comfortable expressing their thoughts and ideas, even unconventional ones, creativity flourishes in such an environment. Emotional leadership fosters this open environment, leading to more innovative solutions.

- Improved Conflict Resolution: Emotional intelligence empowers leaders to navigate conflict constructively. Leaders focus on solutions, not blame. This minimizes disruption and keeps the team moving forward.

- Reduced Stress and Burnout: A positive and supportive work environment is key to employee well-being. Emotional leadership helps create this environment, leading to reduced stress and burnout among team members.

Emotional leadership is not about being overly emotional or sentimental. It's about using your emotional intelligence to create a work environment where everyone feels valued, respected, and empowered to do their best work.

Integrating Emotional Intelligence into Leadership

Leadership styles are categorized in various ways. Some common models focus on decision-making authority or task orientation. However, emotional leadership adds a new dimension to this understanding. Let's explore how different leadership styles can be viewed through the lens of emotional intelligence:

Authoritative Leadership: This style is characterized by a clear vision, decisive action, and the ability to inspire confidence. When combined with high emotional intelligence, authoritative leaders excel at:

1. Communicating the vision with passion and clarity – They inspire team members to believe in the bigger picture and understand their role in achieving it.

2. Building trust through transparency and emotional honesty – Open communication fosters a sense of security and encourages team members to buy into the leader's vision.

3. Providing constructive feedback and fostering development – Emotionally intelligent leaders offer feedback with empathy and focus on growth, motivating team members to reach their full potential.

Democratic Leadership: This style emphasizes collaboration and participation in decision-making. Emotional intelligence is key for democratic leaders to:

1. Create a safe space for open communication. Team members need to feel comfortable expressing ideas without fear of judgment, fostering a sense of psychological safety.

2. Actively listen and acknowledge diverse perspectives. Leaders with high EQ show genuine interest in their team members' thoughts and feelings, fostering a sense of inclusion.

3. Guide the decision-making process effectively. While encouraging participation, emotionally intelligent leaders can ensure discussions stay focused and lead to clear decisions.

Coaching Leadership: This style focuses on developing individuals and maximizing their potential. Emotional intelligence empowers coaches to:

1. Build strong relationships based on trust and empathy. Understanding their team members' strengths and weaknesses allows them to provide personalized coaching and support.

2. Set challenging but achievable goals. Leaders with high EQ can motivate team members by setting goals that are both ambitious and attainable.

3. Provide constructive feedback and celebrate successes. Effective coaching involves offering specific and actionable feedback, delivered in a way that encourages growth. Equally

important is recognizing and celebrating achievements, which boosts morale and motivation.

Affiliative Leadership: This style prioritizes harmony and building strong relationships within the team. Emotional intelligence is crucial for affiliative leaders to:

1. Create a positive and supportive work environment. Leaders with high EQ foster a sense of belonging and connection within the team.

2. Recognize and appreciate individual contributions. Feeling valued motivates team members and fosters a spirit of collaboration.

3. Manage conflict constructively. Emotional intelligence allows leaders to navigate disagreements effectively, focusing on solutions rather than blame.

Pacesetting Leadership: This style focuses on setting high standards and driving results. Emotional intelligence helps pacesetting leaders to:

1. Lead by example – Demonstrating a strong work ethic and commitment to excellence inspires team members to strive for their best.

2. Provide clear expectations and performance metrics. Knowing what's expected and how success is measured keeps teams focused and motivated.

3. Recognize and reward high performance. Acknowledging achievement reinforces positive behaviors and motivates continued excellence.

It's important to remember that these leadership styles are not mutually exclusive. Effective leaders often utilize a blend of styles, adapting their approach based on the situation and the needs of their team. Emotional intelligence empowers them to do this effectively, fostering a dynamic and high-performing team environment.

Strategies for Integrating Emotional Intelligence into Leadership

Emotional intelligence involves recognizing others' emotions and understanding your own. Effective emotional leadership hinges on two crucial pillars: self-awareness and self-regulation. These skills empower you to build strong relationships. They also help you lead with empathy.

Knowing Yourself: The Power of Self-Awareness

Self-awareness is the foundation of emotional intelligence. It involves understanding your emotions, their triggers, and their impact on your behaviour. As a leader, this awareness allows you to:

1. Recognize your strengths and weaknesses: Knowing your limitations allows you to delegate tasks effectively and seek support when needed. It also helps you capitalize on your strengths to inspire and motivate your team.

2. Identify emotional triggers: Certain situations or personalities might evoke strong emotions in you. Recognize triggers to manage reactions and respond thoughtfully, not impulsively.

3. Communicate: When you understand your own emotions, you can express them genuinely. This fosters trust and transparency with your team members.

Mastering Your Emotions: The Art of Self-Regulation

Self-regulation is the ability to manage your emotions effectively. It's not about suppressing emotions, but rather about learning to express them in a constructive manner. As an emotionally intelligent leader, you can:

1. Stay calm under pressure: Maintaining your composure during challenging situations allows you to make clear decisions and offer support to your team. This fosters a sense of security and trust.

2. Manage conflict constructively: When disagreements arise, self-regulation allows you to approach the situation calmly, focusing on solutions rather than assigning blame.

3. Lead by example: Demonstrating emotional control sets a positive tone for your team. When team members see their

leader manage stress effectively, they're more likely to adopt similar behaviors.

Leading with Empathy

Empathy is the cornerstone of emotional intelligence and leadership. It goes beyond simply acknowledging someone's emotions; it's about truly understanding their perspective and feelings. By leading with empathy, you can:

1. Build stronger relationships: When team members feel understood and valued, they're more likely to be engaged and motivated.

2. Make more inclusive decisions: Considering different perspectives allows for more informed decision-making that benefits the entire team.

3. Foster a supportive work environment: Empathy allows you to create a space where team members feel comfortable sharing concerns and seeking help.

Tania Singer, a researcher at the University of California, Berkeley, found that empathy activates brain regions linked to compassion and caregiving. This neurological response can foster a sense of trust and cooperation, essential for building a thriving team.

Developing Your Empathy Muscle

Empathy, like other aspects of emotional intelligence, can be developed. Here are some tips:

1. Practice active listening: Pay close attention to both verbal and nonverbal cues when someone is communicating.

2. Put yourself in their shoes: Try to see things from their perspective and understand their challenges.

Ask open-ended questions: Encourage open communication and allow team members to express their feelings.

3. By prioritizing self-awareness, self-regulation, and empathy, you lay the foundation for emotionally intelligent leadership. These skills empower you to build trust, foster collaboration, and create a work environment where everyone feels valued and empowered to do their best work.

Integrating Empathy into Decision-Making

Leaders often make decisions that impact the lives of their team members. Incorporating empathy improves decision-making. It creates a supportive, inclusive workplace.

Here are some tips:

1. Gather Diverse Perspectives: Don't make decisions in a vacuum. Seek input from your team members and consider the potential impact of your choices on everyone involved.

2. Consider the Emotional Impact: Think beyond the practical implications of your decisions. How might they affect the morale, stress levels, and well-being of your team?

3. Communicate Clearly and Openly: Explain your decisions and the reasoning behind them. Be open to feedback and willing to adjust your course if necessary.

Balancing Vulnerability and Authority

Balancing vulnerability and authority as a leader means being strong and compassionate. This involves being decisive and empathetic.

Emotional leadership thrives on trust. Team members trust their leader. They feel safe expressing themselves, taking risks, and collaborating effectively. This trust is built through transparency – the willingness to share information openly and honestly.

Vulnerability: Not Weakness, But Strength

Leadership has been associated with strength and infallibility. However, emotional leadership flips this script. Being vulnerable, such as admitting mistakes or sharing personal experiences, helps you create a more human connection with your team. This vulnerability fosters trust and encourages others to be open and honest as well.

The University of California, Berkeley study found that teams rated leaders showing vulnerability as more competent and effective. This highlights the power of vulnerability in building trust and fostering a positive work environment.

Putting Transparency and Vulnerability into Practice

1. Admit Mistakes: Don't shy away from owning up to errors in judgment. Acknowledge your mistakes and explain the lessons learned. This shows your team that you're human and allows them to learn from your experiences.

2. Share Information Openly: Keep your team informed about project developments, challenges, and even setbacks. This transparency fosters trust and empowers them to contribute effectively.

3. Celebrate Wins (and Learn from Losses): Acknowledge and celebrate successes with your team. Equally important, be open about setbacks and use them as learning opportunities. This shows authenticity and encourages your team to learn from both positive and negative experiences.

The Ripple Effect of Emotional Leadership: Shaping a Positive Workplace Culture

Emotional leadership doesn't exist in a vacuum. When leaders cultivate self-awareness, empathy, and navigate vulnerability effectively, it creates a ripple effect impacting the entire team and organizational culture.

- Increased Psychological Safety: By fostering trust and openness, emotional leadership creates a space where team members feel safe to take risks and share ideas without fear of judgment. This psychological safety is crucial for innovation and high performance [2].

- Enhanced Collaboration: When team members trust and respect each other, collaboration becomes more natural. Open communication and a shared sense of purpose pave the way for effective teamwork.

- Improved Employee Engagement: Emotional leadership fosters a more positive and supportive work environment, leading to increased employee engagement and reduced turnover. Employees who feel valued and appreciated are more likely to be invested in their work.

- A Culture of Continuous Learning: Transparency and vulnerability allow for open feedback and facilitate a culture of continuous learning. Mistakes become learning experiences, and team members are encouraged to grow and develop their skills.

Emotional leadership isn't about micromanaging emotions or creating a space of emotional chaos. It's about striking a balance between authority and vulnerability, fostering a positive work environment, and empowering your team to achieve great things.

By cultivating emotional intelligence and utilizing the strategies outlined in this chapter, you can become a leader who inspires trust, ignites creativity, and builds a thriving team culture.

Cultivating Emotional Leadership in Your Team

Leadership Self-Assessment: Begin by reflecting on your leadership style. What are your strengths? Where do you see opportunities for growth? Delve into your emotional intelligence, evaluating how well you understand and manage your own emotions, as well as those of others. Use tools like self-reflection journals or leadership assessment surveys to gain insights into your leadership approach.

Team Collaboration Challenge: Now, it's time to put your insights into action. Propose a challenge within your team that focuses on implementing emotional intelligence practices. Encourage open communication, active listening, and empathy. Foster an environment where team members feel comfortable expressing their emotions and opinions. Track the impact of these initiatives on collaboration, productivity, and overall team dynamics. Remember, true leadership isn't about commanding from the top—it's about empowering others to shine and thrive collaboratively. Take the first step towards becoming the emotionally intelligent leader your team deserves.

Key Takeaways

- Understand the essence and importance of emotional leadership in shaping organizational dynamics.

- Demonstrate the practical techniques for infusing emotional intelligence into your leadership style, enhancing team performance and cohesion.

- Master the balance between vulnerability and authority, fostering trust and respect within your team.

- Recognize the profound influence of emotional leadership on organizational culture, driving positivity and productivity.

- Embrace your role as an agent of change, empowered to cultivate a positive work environment through emotional intelligence.

- Reflect on your leadership style, identifying strengths and areas for growth in emotional intelligence.

- Propose initiatives within your team to implement emotional intelligence practices, fostering collaboration and growth.

- Embrace a lifelong journey of learning and development in emotional leadership, recognizing its transformative potential.

- Take solid steps to integrate emotional intelligence into your leadership approach, catalyzing positive change and fostering a culture of empowerment.

Embrace the transformative power of emotional leadership. Start implementing these steps today. Cultivate a positive work environment and empower your team for success.

Reflect on your emotional intelligence strengths and growth areas using the self-assessment tool. Challenge your team to practice active listening and witness the power of empathetic communication.

Chapter 7: Nurturing Collaborative Workspaces

The modern workplace thrives on collaboration. Teams that function cohesively achieve more, solve problems efficiently, and foster a sense of shared purpose. The American Psychological Association states that a collaborative team is likely to see a 24% increase in innovation. Additionally, they may experience a 33% improvement in problem-solving skills and increased job satisfaction.

A cohesive team uses diverse perspectives, encourages innovation, and faces challenges directly. Here, vulnerability is not a weakness but a catalyst for growth.

This chapter explores how effective communication creates collaborative workspaces.

Effective communication goes beyond simply conveying information. It acknowledges feelings, fosters empathy, and creates a safe space for open communication.

This chapter explores how collaborative environments impact productivity. This chapter gives you strategies to improve communication. It helps your team work better together.

Understanding the Role of Effective Communication in Teamwork

Communication is the lifeblood of teamwork. It allows team members to share ideas, solve problems, and work towards a common goal. But effective communication goes beyond simply conveying information.

Effective teamwork goes beyond simply exchanging information. It's a dynamic dance that considers both the what and the how of communication. Traditional communication focuses on the message itself: the facts, figures, and instructions. Emotional communication, however, acknowledges the emotional undercurrents that influence how messages are received and interpreted.

Here's how effective communication influences teamwork:

1. Building Trust: Clear and open communication fosters trust within the team. When team members feel their voices are heard and their ideas valued, they're more likely to collaborate effectively.

2. Enhancing Understanding: Effective communication encourages team members to consider diverse perspectives and gain a deeper understanding of the issues at hand. This fosters a more collaborative and inclusive work environment.

3. Promoting Active Listening: Effective communication requires active listening, where you truly focus on understanding the speaker's message, both verbal and nonverbal. This builds trust and ensures everyone feels heard and valued.

4. Navigating Conflict Constructively: Disagreements are inevitable in any team. Effective communication allows for conflict to be addressed constructively, focusing on finding solutions rather than assigning blame.

Research backs the positive impact of collaborative work environments. The American Psychological Association study found that effective teams enjoy various benefits, such as:

1. Increased Innovation: Collaboration fosters a cross-pollination of ideas, leading to more creative and innovative solutions.

2. Enhanced Problem-Solving: Diverse perspectives within a team allow for a more comprehensive understanding of challenges and the development of more effective solutions.

3. Improved Job Satisfaction: Feeling valued, supported, and heard within a collaborative team contributes to increased job satisfaction and motivation.

4. Boosted Productivity: When team members work together effectively, communication is streamlined, tasks are delegated efficiently, and overall productivity increases.

Collaboration achieves results. It fosters belonging and a shared purpose. Team members who openly express themselves create a positive work experience. Team members who work together towards a common goal also contribute to this positive experience. This experience is rewarding. Collaboration motivates individuals and teams, making the workforce more engaged and productive.

Practical Tips for Effective Communication

Now that we understand the power of effective communication, let's explore some practical tips for integrating it into your daily interactions:

1. Clarity is Key: Present information clearly, concisely, and in a way that is easy for everyone to understand. Avoid jargon and technical terms whenever possible.

2. Embrace Transparency: Share information openly and honestly, fostering trust within the team. Explain the reasoning behind decisions and keep everyone informed about progress.

3. Pay Attention: Being attentive to both verbal and nonverbal cues, and ask clarifying questions to ensure understanding. Put away distractions and make eye contact to show you're fully engaged.

4. Emphasize Empathy: Try to see things from the other person's perspective and acknowledge their feelings. A simple phrase like "It sounds like you're concerned about..." can go a long way.

5. Encourage Two-Way Communication: Create a space where everyone feels comfortable sharing their ideas and feedback. This fosters a more collaborative and inclusive environment.

By incorporating these practices, you can create a foundation for effective communication that empowers your team to collaborate effectively and achieve remarkable results.

Challenges in Fostering Effective Communication at Work

We've established the power of effective communication in fostering a collaborative and successful team environment. But truly, clear and open communication doesn't always happen naturally in the workplace. As effective communication is the cornerstone of successful teamwork, there can be challenges that hinder effective communication in workplaces.

Communication Barriers

1. Fear of Judgment: A major barrier is the fear of being criticized or appearing incompetent. Studies by the University of California, Berkeley, show that this fear can lead to employees withholding valuable ideas and hindering innovation. Creating a safe space for open dialogue and acknowledging the value of diverse perspectives is crucial to overcoming this barrier.

2. Lack of Trust: Without trust, collaboration crumbles. A study published in Harvard Business Review highlights the connection between trust and effective communication within teams. Building trust takes time and requires consistent effort. Leaders who demonstrate transparency, keep their promises, and value team members' input foster a foundation of trust.

3. Misunderstandings: Nonverbal cues, cultural differences, and communication styles can all lead to misunderstandings. Research by the International Journal of Business Communication emphasizes the importance of clear and concise communication, coupled with active listening, to bridge these gaps.

4. Information Overload: In today's fast-paced work environment, information overload is a real concern. A study by the American Psychological Association reveals that constant emails, messages, and meetings can make it difficult to focus on and absorb important information. Prioritizing communication channels, setting clear expectations for response times, and encouraging focused meetings can help alleviate information overload.

5. Conflicting Communication Styles: We all have preferred communication styles; some are direct and concise, while others are more indirect and nuanced. A study by Personality and Social Psychology Bulletin suggests that recognizing these differences and adapting your communication style accordingly can improve understanding and collaboration.

Building the Bridge to Collaboration

So, how do we overcome these challenges and build a culture of effective communication? Here are some evidence-based strategies:

1. Be an Example: Leaders set the tone for the team culture. By demonstrating effective communication skills—active listening, clear communication, and empathy—leaders create a model for others to follow. Research by Gallup highlights the link between strong leadership communication and employee engagement.

2. Invest in Team Building: Well-designed team-building activities can be powerful tools for fostering trust, communication, and collaboration. A study published in the International Journal of Business and Management found that team-building activities that encourage teamwork on challenging tasks or promote shared laughter can break down barriers and build stronger bonds within the team.

3. Embrace Transparency: Open and honest communication builds trust. Share information about company goals, project updates, and decision-making processes with the team. A study by the Society for Human Resource Management highlights the importance of transparency in building trust and fostering a positive work environment.

4. Provide Training: Invest in communication skills training for your team. This can help team members develop their active listening skills, assertive communication techniques, and conflict resolution strategies. Research by the American Society

for Training and Development shows that communication skills training can lead to improved teamwork and overall job performance.

Creating a Culture of Emotional Support

Collaboration thrives in an environment where team members feel not just valued for their skills, but also supported on a human level.

Leadership Influence

Leaders play a pivotal role in fostering a culture of emotional support. Their actions and behaviors set the tone for the entire team. Here's how effective leaders cultivate this vital aspect of collaboration:

1. Leading by Example: Leaders who embody emotional intelligence demonstrate empathy, active listening, and open communication. It has been found that leaders who display emotional intelligence foster trust and psychological safety within their teams, leading to increased innovation and collaboration.

2. Promoting Open Communication: Leaders who promote open communication create a space for team members to comfortably share ideas, concerns, and frustrations. Holding regular team meetings with open agendas, actively soliciting

feedback, and practicing active listening are ways leaders can achieve this. The Society for Human Resource Management (SHRM) research confirms open communication drives employee engagement and job satisfaction.

3. Building Trust: Trust is the foundation of any strong team. Leaders can build trust by being transparent, keeping their promises, and acknowledging team members' contributions. A meta-analysis published in the Journal of Applied Psychology found a strong correlation between trust and team performance.

4. Celebrating Achievements—Big and Small: Recognition goes a long way in fostering a supportive environment. Leaders can celebrate both individual and team achievements, big or small. This reinforces positive behaviors and motivates team members to continue contributing their best work. Research by the Achievers Workforce Institute highlights the link between employee recognition and increased engagement, productivity, and retention.

5. Providing Constructive Feedback: Leaders who provide constructive feedback, focused on behavior and offering specific suggestions for improvement, empower their team members to learn and grow. A study published in the Harvard Business Review emphasizes the importance of creating a "growth mindset" within teams, where challenges are seen as opportunities for development.

These leadership actions create a safe space for team members to be themselves, openly express their emotions, and collaborate effectively.

Team-Building Exercises: Cultivating the Soil of Collaboration

Team-building exercises are more than just a fun office activity. When strategically chosen, they can be powerful tools for fostering trust, empathy, and open communication—the essential ingredients for emotional support. Here are some effective exercises:

1. Strengths-Based Activities: These activities help team members identify and appreciate each other's strengths. One simple exercise involves having each team member write down their top three strengths and then sharing them with the group. This fosters understanding and appreciation for the unique value each person brings to the team.

2. Shared Challenges: Exercises that involve working together to overcome a common challenge can be a powerful way to build trust and communication. Escape room challenges or collaborative problem-solving activities encourage teamwork and communication in a fun and engaging setting.

3. Volunteer Activities: Giving back to the community through volunteer work can be a rewarding experience that strengthens team bonds. Working together towards a common goal outside the traditional work environment fosters empathy and understanding. A study by the Corporation for National Service found that volunteerism can lead to increased collaboration and communication skills within teams.

4. Open Communication Games: Games that encourage open communication and active listening can help team members feel more comfortable expressing themselves. One example is "Two Truths and a Lie," where each team member shares three statements, two of which are true and one is a lie. The others have to guess which statement is the lie. This lighthearted activity can help break down communication barriers and encourage team members to listen attentively.

By prioritizing emotional support through strong leadership and strategic team-building exercises, you cultivate an environment where individuals feel valued, heard, and empowered. This collaborative ecosystem allows diverse perspectives to flourish, fostering creativity, innovation, and ultimately, remarkable results. The next section dives deeper into the specific strategies team members can adopt to foster emotional support within their teams. We'll explore communication techniques, conflict resolution approaches, and the power of active listening to build a truly collaborative team.

The Pillars of Individual EQ

Emotional intelligence equips you with the skills to navigate team dynamics effectively. Here's how you can leverage your EQ to contribute to a high-functioning team:

- Self-Awareness: This involves understanding your emotions, how they influence your thoughts and actions, and how you perceive yourself. Self-aware team members can recognize their strengths and weaknesses, and adjust their behavior accordingly to contribute effectively in different situations.

- Self-Regulation: This refers to your ability to manage your emotions effectively. Emotionally intelligent team members can manage stress, control impulses, and stay calm under pressure. This allows them to navigate challenging situations constructively and avoid letting emotions cloud their judgment.

- Social Awareness: This is the ability to understand the emotions, needs, and perspectives of others. Socially aware team members can empathize with colleagues, build rapport, and foster a sense of trust and connection within the team.

- Relationship Management: This involves building and maintaining positive relationships. Emotionally intelligent team members communicate effectively, handle conflict constructively, and collaborate effectively with others.

- Motivation: This refers to your intrinsic drive to achieve goals. Highly motivated team members are passionate about their work and inspire others with their enthusiasm.

Emotional Intelligence for Conflict Resolution

Disagreements are inevitable in any team setting. But for high-performing teams, conflict becomes an opportunity for growth and innovation, not a roadblock to progress. Emotional intelligence (EQ) plays a crucial role in navigating these situations constructively.

Here are some strategies that leverage emotional intelligence for effective conflict resolution:

1. Self-Management: The Art of Staying Calm

Emotional intelligence isn't just about understanding others' emotions; it's also about managing your own. During conflict, self-management is critical. Techniques like deep breathing, taking a short break, or mentally reframing the situation can help you approach the conversation with a cooler head. By managing your own emotions, you can avoid escalating the situation and create a space for productive dialogue.

2. Empathy: Stepping into Another's Shoes

A core component of emotional intelligence is empathy—the ability to understand and share the feelings of another person. In conflict resolution, empathy allows you to see the situation from your teammate's perspective. Actively listen to their concerns, acknowledge their feelings, and validate their point of view. This fosters trust and creates a collaborative environment where solutions can be found.

3. Communication: Finding Common Ground

Clear and concise communication is essential for resolving conflict. Express your own feelings and needs. Focus on the issue at hand, avoiding personal attacks or blame games. By communicating effectively, you can bridge the gap between perspectives and find common ground.

Building a Culture of Mutual Respect

By integrating these emotional intelligence strategies, teams can transform conflict from a disruptive force into a catalyst for growth. Remember, fostering a culture of mutual respect is key. Treat each other with respect, even during disagreements. This allows for open communication, honest feedback, and ultimately, a stronger, more collaborative team.

Putting EQ into Action

Here are some practical strategies to integrate emotional intelligence into your daily team interactions:

- Active Listening: Give your full attention to your team members when they speak. Understand the person's message, ask clarifying questions if needed, and avoid interrupting. This demonstrates respect and encourages open communication.

- Empathy in Action: Put yourself in your colleagues' shoes. Try to understand their perspectives and challenges. Phrases like "It sounds like you're concerned about X" show empathy and build trust.

117

- Positive Communication: Be expressive about your needs and concerns. Avoid accusatory language and focus on finding solutions. Positive communication fosters collaboration and reduces defensiveness.

- Celebrate Diverse Perspectives: Don't shy away from expressing your ideas, but also appreciate the value of different viewpoints. Ask questions to understand differing opinions and explore how they can strengthen the team's approach.

This chapter equips you, the conductor, with the tools to cultivate emotional intelligence within your team, leading them towards a collaborative masterpiece.

Tuning In: Diagnosing Your Team's EQ

It is imperative to have a thorough understanding of your subordinate's present situation before assuming leadership.

Here's a diagnostic approach to assessing your team's emotional intelligence:

Step 1:

Pay attention to team meetings. Are discussions dominated by a few voices? Do emotions run high, hindering progress? These steps might indicate a lack of self-awareness or social awareness within the team.

Step 2:

Observe team dynamics. Do members work well together or exhibit solo acts? A prevalence of solo acts might suggest challenges with relationship management or a lack of shared motivation.

Step 3:

Analyze project outcomes. Does the team consistently miss deadlines or fail to meet goals? Poor performance could be a sign of underlying emotional intelligence issues impacting collaboration and overall effectiveness.

Once you've diagnosed your team's EQ strengths and weaknesses, it's time to conduct them towards a collaborative masterpiece.

Here are some actionable steps:

The Self-Awareness Exercises

Encourage team members to reflect on their strengths and weaknesses through personality quizzes or journaling exercises. This self-awareness is the foundation for individual and collective emotional intelligence.

The Emotional Intelligence Training

Invest in workshops on emotional intelligence and conflict resolution. Equip your team with the tools to manage emotions, navigate interpersonal challenges, and build stronger relationships.

Your Role

As the leader, embody emotional intelligence. Practice active listening, acknowledge emotions, and manage conflict constructively. Your actions set the tone for the entire team.

1. Foster open and honest communication by creating a safe space for team members to share ideas and concerns. Hold regular meetings with clear agendas that encourage active participation from all members.

2. Celebrate the unique perspectives and experiences each team member brings to the table. Encourage respectful dialogue and value the power of diverse viewpoints in fostering innovation.

3. Build an environment of safety where team members feel safe to take risks, share ideas, and admit mistakes. Encourage experimentation, acknowledge effort, and celebrate learning from mistakes.

4. Recognize and appreciate team members who display emotional intelligence in their interactions with others. Public recognition or incentive programs can reinforce the importance of these skills.

5. Organize team-building activities that promote trust, communication, and collaboration. Consider activities that encourage teamwork on challenging tasks or promote shared laughter and camaraderie.

Developing emotional intelligence as a team is an ongoing process. Consistently implement these strategies. Create a culture fostering collaboration. Empower individuals. Allow your team to perform at its peak. Embrace the journey, and together, create a collaborative symphony that surpasses all expectations.

Key Takeaways

- Emotional communication significantly influences teamwork dynamics, fostering trust and cohesion among team members.

- Addressing common barriers to emotional communication, such as fear of vulnerability, is essential for cultivating a collaborative workspace.

- Effective leadership plays a pivotal role in creating a culture of emotional support and collaboration within teams.

- Embrace the unique perspectives and experiences each team member brings to the table. A variety of viewpoints fuels creativity and innovation.

- Create an environment where team members feel safe to take risks, share ideas, and admit mistakes without fear of punishment. This psychological safety fosters trust and collaboration.

- Open and honest communication is the cornerstone of collaborative workspaces. When team members feel safe to share ideas and concerns, innovation flourishes, and problems are solved more effectively.

- Disagreements are inevitable, but with emotional intelligence, they can become opportunities for growth. By managing emotions, practicing empathy, and focusing on solutions, teams can navigate conflict productively.

We've seen how emotional intelligence builds successful team harmony. Remember, a collaborative team requires consistent effort, open communication, and a commitment to fostering emotional well-being.

The next chapter delves into a crucial aspect of emotional intelligence – individual awareness. We'll explore the concept of traditional masculinity and its impact on emotional expression. The chapter explores how ingrained stereotypes affect relationships, personal development, and societal expectations. Gain insights to challenge outdated norms and promote inclusivity and authenticity. These strategies are practical and valuable for all aspects of life.

Part 3: Shaping a Stronger Identity through Sensitivity

Chapter 8: Deconstructing Traditional Masculinity

In a world where societal norms often dictate gender roles and expectations, the concept of masculinity has long been confined to a narrow and rigid definition. However, as we evolve as a society, it becomes increasingly apparent that these traditional notions of masculinity are not only outdated but have done more harm than good.

This chapter challenges traditional masculinity. The journey is thought-provoking. By examining the societal constructs that have shaped our understanding of what it means to be a man, we aim to pave the way for a more authentic and inclusive identity. It's time to question the stereotypes, stigmas, and expectations placed upon men and to embrace a broader spectrum of masculinity—one that celebrates diversity, vulnerability, and emotional authenticity. This exploration empowers individuals to break free from traditional masculinity. It helps them embrace a more liberated sense of self. Delve into masculinity complexities.

Analyzing the Limitations of Conventional Masculinity

Societal Expectations

Boys are taught traditional masculinity traits like strength, stoicism, and dominance from a young age. Society expects men to follow norms. These are reinforced by media, peer pressure, and stereotypes. Pressure to conform can create a rigid framework. It restricts men from exploring their identity. Men can't express themselves authentically. Men who closely follow traditional masculine norms are more prone to mental health problems like depression, anxiety, and substance abuse.

Impact on Emotional Expression

The pressure to conform to traditional masculinity can have a profound impact on a man's emotional well-being in several ways.

When boys are discouraged from expressing a full range of emotions, they develop a limited emotional vocabulary. This makes it difficult for them to identify and communicate their feelings effectively, leading to frustration and misunderstandings in relationships. Imagine trying to navigate a complex situation with only a handful of words to describe your internal state.

Difficulty with Vulnerability: Traditional masculinity often equates vulnerability with weakness. This makes it challenging for men to open up about their struggles, seek support, or build deep, emotionally intimate connections. Without vulnerability, relationships can become superficial and lack the trust and understanding needed to truly thrive.

The "Man Box": The concept of the "man box" refers to the narrow range of emotions and behaviors deemed acceptable for men. This box can be stifling, preventing men from exploring their full potential and expressing themselves authentically. It's like being forced to wear a suit that's several sizes too small; it restricts movement and hinders your ability to function at your best.

The Cost of Emotional Suppression

The impact of adhering to traditional masculinity goes beyond just emotional well-being. Here's a look at the toll conventional masculinity, which often discourages emotional expression, can take on men's well-being:

- Mental Health Burdens: Studies show men are less likely to seek help for mental health issues. Bottling emotions can lead to anxiety, depression, and even physical health problems.

- Strained Relationships: Difficulty expressing emotions can create distance in relationships. Partners may feel disconnected or unheard, leading to conflict and dissatisfaction.

- Fatherhood Impediments: Emotional suppression can hinder a father's ability to connect with his children. Children need dads who can validate their feelings and model healthy emotional expression.

- Missed Opportunities for Growth: Suppressing emotions limits your ability to learn and grow. By opening up about challenges and failures, you can gain valuable insights and build resilience.

- A Life Half-Lived: Living in fear of expressing emotions can rob you of a fulfilling life. Vulnerability allows you to experience joy, love, and connection more deeply.

By breaking free from the constraints of traditional masculinity, men can cultivate greater emotional resilience, healthier relationships, and a more authentic sense of self. It's time to liberate ourselves from outdated gender norms and embrace a more inclusive and compassionate vision of masculinity.

Challenging Conventional Beliefs

Men should be able to express their emotions freely, pursue interests traditionally deemed "feminine," and prioritize mental well-being without facing social stigma. Men experience emotions just as intensely as women do. Yet, societal norms dictate that they suppress these feelings. Why? Because vulnerability is seen as weakness, true strength lies in acknowledging our emotions, not in bottling them up. When we allow ourselves to feel, we become more authentic and more human.

Men who defy the stoic stereotype often suffer in silence. They grapple with anxiety, depression, and loneliness, afraid to seek help. Why? Because admitting vulnerability feels like a betrayal of their masculinity. But it's time to rewrite the script.

Questioning What You Believe

Masculinity isn't monolithic. It's a spectrum that encompasses a diverse range of emotions, behaviours, and interests. Yet, stereotypes paint a narrow picture: men are stoic, emotionless, and aggressive. But are these truly the only facets of masculinity? Here's how to challenge these ingrained beliefs:

- Interrogate Your Assumptions: Reflect on your own beliefs about masculinity. Where did they come from? Are they based on societal expectations or your personal values? Challenge any limiting stereotypes you hold about yourself or other men.

- Expand Your Horizons: Seek out positive portrayals of men who defy traditional masculinity. Look for books, movies, and TV shows that feature male characters who express a full range of emotions and interests.

- The Power of "And": Masculinity doesn't have to be an "either/or" proposition. You can be strong and compassionate, assertive and nurturing. Embrace the concept of "and" to create a more holistic definition of masculinity that aligns with your values.

The Stigma Factor: Breaking Down the Barriers

Men who deviate from traditional masculinity often face social stigma. They may be labeled as "weak," "effeminate," or "not a real man." This stigma can be isolating and discourage men from expressing themselves authentically. Here's why dismantling the stigma is crucial:

- The Cost of Conformity: Conforming to unrealistic expectations can lead to a disconnect from one's authentic self. This can have a negative impact on mental health and overall well-being.

- Silencing Vulnerability: The stigma against emotional expression prevents men from seeking help when they need it. Creating a space for open communication about emotions is vital for men's mental health.

- A Missed Opportunity for Connection: When men feel pressured to conform, they miss out on the richness of human connection that comes from authentic expression.

Building a More Accepting World: Practical Steps

We can all play a role in dismantling the stigma surrounding non-traditional masculinity. Here are some ways to contribute:

- Challenge Sexist Jokes and Comments: Don't let sexist jokes or comments go unchecked. Speak up and challenge these harmful stereotypes.

- Celebrate Diversity: Actively celebrate men who defy traditional masculinity. Let them know their authentic expression is valued and appreciated.

- Lead by Example: Embrace your own emotional vulnerability and challenge traditional gender roles in your own life. This sets a positive example for others.

Embracing Authenticity: The Power of Being You

Moving beyond stereotypes opens the door to a more fulfilling experience of masculinity. Here's what you gain by embracing your authentic self:

- Improved Mental Health: Expressing emotions in a healthy way can reduce stress, anxiety, and depression.

- Stronger Relationships: Being vulnerable allows you to build deeper, more meaningful connections with others.

- A Life Lived on Your Terms: When you break free from societal expectations, you can live a life that aligns with your values and aspirations.

Encouraging Authentic Self-Expression

Strength Beyond the Stereotype

The traditional view of masculinity depicts men as emotionless and strong. While emotional control and resilience are certainly valuable traits, this narrow definition excludes a vast spectrum of what it means to be a man.

Here's why celebrating this diversity is crucial:

Strength Comes in Many Forms: Physical strength is just one facet of masculinity. Emotional intelligence, compassion, and vulnerability are equally important qualities. Embracing diverse expressions helps men become well-rounded individuals. They can navigate life's complexities with a broader skillset.

Beyond the Binary: Masculinity doesn't exist in opposition to femininity. It exists on a spectrum, allowing men to incorporate traditionally "feminine" traits like nurturing and creativity into their identity. This broader definition fosters a more inclusive vision of masculinity that allows all men to feel like they belong.

Breaking Free from Limitations: The limitations of traditional masculinity can hinder personal growth. Embracing diverse expressions allows men to explore different interests and activities, leading to a more fulfilling life. A man enjoys rock climbing and tending to his garden. Both activities can boost self-esteem and well-being through diverse expressions of masculinity.

The Benefits of Diversity in Masculinity

Studies have shown a clear link between embracing diverse expressions of masculinity and positive outcomes for men. In 2018, the Journal of Counseling Psychology published a study. It found that men with flexible masculinity views had better self-esteem and life satisfaction. Additionally, a 2020 study in the Psychology of Men and Masculinity found that men who felt comfortable expressing a wider range of emotions had stronger social relationships.

Impact on Mental Health

The restrictive nature of traditional masculinity can have a profound impact on men's mental health.

- Emotional Suppression and its Toll: Discouraging men from expressing a full range of emotions leads to emotional suppression. This can manifest as stress, anxiety, and difficulty coping with challenges. Unexpressed emotions don't disappear; they fester and can lead to outbursts of anger or difficulty managing emotions in healthy ways.

- Be a Loner: The image of the self-sufficient, independent man can be isolating. It discourages men from seeking help or building strong support networks, hindering their emotional well-being. Men who struggle to connect and share their burdens are more susceptible to feelings of loneliness and depression.

- The Pressure to Conform: The pressure to conform to a narrow definition of masculinity can create immense internal conflict. Men who feel they don't measure up to the stereotype may experience feelings of inadequacy and shame, further impacting their mental health.

Promoting Emotional Resilience

Building Emotional Resilience

Traditional masculinity discourages men from acknowledging and processing emotions. This leads to a lack of emotional resilience. Men can develop emotional resilience and cope with life's challenges by breaking free from constraints. One effective strategy is to practice mindfulness and emotional awareness. Men can deepen their self-understanding by being attentive to thoughts and feelings without judgment.

Another crucial aspect of building emotional resilience is developing healthy coping mechanisms. Instead of resorting to harmful behaviors like substance abuse or aggression to numb their emotions, men can explore constructive outlets such as journaling, exercise, or engaging in hobbies they enjoy. These activities not only provide a healthy release for pent-up emotions but also promote overall well-being.

Seeking professional help through therapy or counseling can be immensely beneficial. A trained therapist can provide guidance and support in navigating complex emotions, offering tools and techniques to enhance emotional resilience. Participating in support groups or men's circles can create a sense of community and validation. This normalizes the experience of emotional vulnerability.

Empowering Vulnerability

Contrary to the belief that vulnerability is a sign of weakness, embracing vulnerability can actually contribute to emotional strength and well-being. When men allow themselves to be vulnerable, they create authentic connections with others and foster deeper intimacy in their relationships.

To empower vulnerability, men can start by challenging the societal norms that equate vulnerability with weakness. Instead, they can reframe vulnerability as an act of courage and authenticity. By sharing their thoughts, feelings, and struggles with trusted friends or partners, men can cultivate a sense of belonging and support that bolsters their emotional resilience.

Practicing self-compassion is essential to embracing vulnerability. Men should learn to treat themselves with kindness and understanding, especially during times of distress or failure. By embracing their imperfections and acknowledging their humanity, men can develop a stronger sense of self-worth and resilience in the face of adversity.

In summary, promoting emotional resilience involves breaking free from the constraints of traditional masculinity and embracing vulnerability as a source of strength. By cultivating emotional awareness, healthy coping mechanisms, and self-compassion, men can build the resilience needed to navigate life's challenges with grace and authenticity.

Some inspiring journeys of individuals who have deconstructed traditional masculinity and embraced a more authentic way of being highlight the positive outcomes of this transformation.

From Wrestler to Therapist: The Evolution of Glenn Stanton

Glenn Stanton was once known as "Stone Cold" Steve Austin, a larger-than-life professional wrestler. His on-screen persona embodied the traditional image of masculinity – tough, aggressive, and stoic. However, after retiring from wrestling, Stanton embarked on a surprising journey. He returned to school to become a therapist; a profession often stereotyped as "feminine." This career shift sparked criticism, but Stanton remained undeterred. In an interview with The Guardian, he stated, "Being a man isn't about how tough you are... It's about being there for people, being present, and being vulnerable." Stanton's journey exemplifies the power of breaking free from stereotypes and pursuing a path that aligns with one's values.

It's inspiring to see someone challenge societal norms and embrace a different path, regardless of expectations. Stanton's journey reminds us that true strength lies in compassion, empathy, and authenticity.

From Football Field to Fashion Icon: The Duality of Harry Styles

Harry Styles, a former member of the boy band One Direction, has become a cultural icon known for his flamboyant fashion sense and emotional vulnerability. He regularly challenges traditional notions of masculinity by wearing clothing typically associated with women, such as dresses and high heels. Despite criticism, Styles remains unapologetically himself. In a 2020 interview with Vogue, he stated, "What's feminine isn't weak and what's masculine isn't strong." Styles' success demonstrates that embracing a more fluid and expressive form of masculinity can be commercially viable and culturally impactful.

From Boardroom to Ballroom: The Artistic Expression of Derek Hough

Derek Hough, a multiple-time champion on the dance competition show "Dancing with the Stars," is another example of a man defying stereotypes. In a world where dance is often seen as a feminine pursuit, Hough excels in a traditionally "feminine" art form while maintaining a strong and confident presence. His artistry and dedication have earned him immense respect and popularity. Hough's story highlights the importance of embracing diverse passions and celebrating artistic expression, regardless of gender norms.

Key Takeaways

- Traditional masculinity norms often constrain men's emotional expression, limiting their ability to fully engage with their feelings and experiences.

- Embracing a broader definition of masculinity challenges stereotypes and fosters emotional well-being, leading to healthier and more fulfilling relationships.

- Recognizing vulnerability as a strength rather than a weakness empowers men to cultivate emotional resilience and navigate life's challenges with authenticity and courage.

- Breaking free from rigid gender expectations allows men to explore and celebrate their unique identities, fostering a sense of self-acceptance and belonging.

- Society's narrow definition of masculinity can contribute to mental health issues such as depression and anxiety, highlighting the importance of promoting diverse expressions of gender identity.

- Encouraging open dialogue about masculinity helps dismantle harmful stereotypes and promotes a culture of acceptance and inclusivity.

- Individuals who challenge traditional masculinity norms often experience greater personal growth and fulfillment as they embrace their authentic selves.

- Building emotional intelligence enables men to cultivate healthier relationships and communicate effectively with others, enriching both personal and professional interactions.

- Embracing vulnerability fosters empathy and compassion, strengthening connections with others and creating a more empathetic society.

- By deconstructing traditional masculinity, men can lead more fulfilling lives, free from the constraints of outdated gender norms, and contribute to a more equitable and inclusive world.

Deconstructing traditional masculinity means breaking free from societal constraints. It also involves embracing authenticity and promoting emotional well-being. Challenging gender norms and celebrating diverse expressions of masculinity can help individuals develop self-awareness, resilience, and compassion. Embracing vulnerability as strength requires courage and self-reflection. The benefits are deeper connections, healthier relationships, and personal fulfillment.

We will continue to explore masculinity further in the next chapter. It will focus on embracing sensitivity as a strength, not a weakness. You will discover how sensitivity can be a source of resilience, empathy, and authentic connection.

Chapter 9: Strength in Sensitivity

In a world where strength is often synonymous with physical prowess or unyielding resilience, it's time to challenge these conventional notions and redefine strength within the realm of emotional vulnerability.

Embracing sensitivity isn't about succumbing to fragility; rather, it's about showing emotions that make us uniquely human.

When we embrace our sensitivity, we open ourselves up to deeper connections with others, fostering empathy, understanding, and compassion. This heightened emotional awareness strengthens our interpersonal relationships.

Embracing sensitivity empowers us to navigate life's complexities with grace and resilience. Rather than viewing sensitivity as a liability, we recognize it as a superpower—an invaluable tool for self-discovery, personal growth, and navigating the world with empathy and compassion.

Strength isn't just about enduring hardships with a stiff upper lip; it's about having the courage to confront our emotions openly and authentically.

True strength lies in our ability to acknowledge our vulnerabilities and face them head-on. It's the courage to express our fears, insecurities, and doubts, even when society tells us to suppress them. By embracing our emotional vulnerability, we demonstrate an unparalleled strength of character—the strength to be true to ourselves, despite the pressures to conform to societal norms.

It takes immense strength to empathize with others, to lend a listening ear, and to offer support in times of need. This kind of strength isn't measured by physical might but by the depth of our compassion and empathy.

Redefining strength in emotional vulnerability empowers us to embrace humanity fully. We believe real strength comes from embracing emotions fully. It's okay to be vulnerable because vulnerability is a powerful strength.

Through this chapter, we'll explore the several ways in which embracing sensitivity can lead to greater fulfilment, resilience, and overall well-being

The Mindset Shift

To find strength in sensitivity, a transformative mindset shift is essential. Traditionally, sensitivity has been stigmatized as a weakness, often associated with vulnerability and fragility. However, to unlock its true potential, men must reframe their perception of sensitivity and recognize it as a profound source of strength.

For many men, sensitivity feels like a double-edged sword. It fosters emotional connections and empathy. However, it may trigger self-doubt and a fear of appearing weak.

The first step towards embracing your sensitivity is to challenge the narrative you've been conditioned to believe. Society often portrays sensitivity as a feminine quality, contrasting it with the supposed "strength" of stoicism.

One effective strategy for shifting our mindset is practicing self-compassion. By treating ourselves with kindness and understanding, we can break free from self-judgment and embrace our sensitivity with greater acceptance.

Men often suppress emotions and conform to stereotypes of toughness and stoicism. By questioning these norms and embracing a more inclusive definition of masculinity, individuals can liberate themselves from the constraints of societal expectations.

It is essential to recognize the inherent value of sensitivity in fostering deeper connections and empathy.

Sensitivity helps individuals understand emotions, fostering better relationships and boosting emotional intelligence. Rather than viewing sensitivity as a liability, men can reframe it as a superpower that enriches their lives and empowers them to navigate the complexities of the human experience with grace and authenticity.

By engaging in mindfulness meditation, individuals can develop a greater awareness of their thoughts and emotions, allowing them to observe without judgment. Self-reflection encourages individuals to examine their beliefs and behaviours, challenging internalized stigma and fostering self-acceptance.

Embracing sensitivity as a source of strength requires courage and vulnerability. It involves stepping into discomfort, dismantling ingrained beliefs, and redefining personal identity. Embarking on this journey unlocks sensitivity's power. Men gain resilience, authenticity, and emotional well-being.

Building Confidence in Expressing Sensitivity

Building confidence in expressing sensitivity requires courage and self-assurance. One powerful approach is to start small by gradually exposing ourselves to situations where we can express our emotions authentically. This might involve sharing our feelings with trusted friends or loved ones, writing in a journal, or engaging in creative outlets such as art or music.

Setting boundaries and advocating for our emotional needs are crucial to building confidence. It's essential to communicate assertively and assertively communicate our boundaries to others, allowing us to honor our emotional well-being while fostering genuine connections.

Research indicates that individuals who embrace their sensitivity and express their emotions authentically experience greater psychological well-being and resilience. By reshaping our personal identity to view sensitivity as a strength and building confidence in expressing it, we empower ourselves to lead more fulfilling and authentic lives. Through this chapter, we'll explore additional strategies for harnessing the power of sensitivity to cultivate resilience, deepen connections, and thrive in a world that celebrates authenticity.

Here are examples of men who have defied stereotypes and discovered immense strength by embracing their sensitivity.

Vulnerability on the Court: Kevin Love, a star athlete in the NBA, shattered traditional expectations by openly discussing his struggles with anxiety and depression. Love's vulnerability resonated with millions, demonstrating that strength lies not in suppressing emotions, but in acknowledging and dealing with them head-on. His courage to share his story inspired countless men to seek help for their own mental health struggles, proving that emotional intelligence and vulnerability are not signs of weakness, but essential tools for a fulfilling life.

Leading with Empathy: Howard Schultz, former CEO of Starbucks, attributes his success to his ability to connect with his employees on an emotional level. Schultz prioritizes empathy and emotional intelligence in leadership, creating a company culture that values open communication and vulnerability. His approach challenges the stereotype of the cold, emotionless

CEO, proving that strong leadership thrives on compassion and understanding.

The Artist's Raw Emotion: John Mayer, a Grammy-winning singer-songwriter, pours his heart and soul into his music. His lyrics explore a range of emotions, from vulnerability and heartbreak to joy and love. Mayer's willingness to express his emotions authentically resonates deeply with fans, proving that sensitivity is not a hindrance to artistic expression, but a powerful source of inspiration.

From Warrior to Healer: Russell Wilson, a star quarterback in the NFL, embodies the evolving definition of masculinity. Beyond his athletic prowess, Wilson is known for his compassion and emotional intelligence. He actively supports mental health initiatives and speaks openly about his faith, challenging the stereotype of the tough, emotionless athlete. Wilson's vulnerability inspires fans and demonstrates that strength comes in many forms, including the courage to be open and caring.

These are just a few examples of men who have redefined strength. Their stories challenge the misconception that sensitivity is a weakness. Instead, they demonstrate that embracing your emotions can lead to deeper connections, greater self-awareness, and ultimately, a richer more fulfilling life.

Self-Care Practices

Self-care practices play a pivotal role in enhancing emotional well-being, particularly for men who embrace sensitivity. By prioritizing self-care, men can nurture their emotional health and embark on a journey of self-discovery that celebrates their sensitivity rather than viewing it as a weakness.

1. Mindfulness Meditation: Engaging in mindfulness meditation allows men to cultivate present-moment awareness and develop a deeper connection with their thoughts and emotions. Through regular practice, individuals can learn to observe their feelings without judgment, fostering self-acceptance and emotional resilience.

2. Journaling: Journaling provides a constructive outlet for men to explore their thoughts and emotions in a safe and private space. By putting pen to paper, individuals can gain insight into their innermost feelings, identify patterns of behaviour, and track their emotional journey over time. Journaling can serve as a powerful tool for self-reflection and self-expression.

3. Creative Expression: Engaging in creative activities such as writing, painting, or playing music can be highly therapeutic for sensitive men. These outlets allow individuals to channel their emotions into artistic expression, providing a sense of catharsis and empowerment. Through creative endeavours, men can tap into their innermost feelings and express them in meaningful and authentic ways.

4. Nature Walks: Spending time in nature offers a respite from the stresses of daily life and allows men to reconnect with their surroundings and themselves. Whether it's a stroll through the woods or a hike in the mountains, immersing oneself in nature can promote relaxation, reduce anxiety, and enhance overall well-being. Nature serves as a powerful healer, providing solace and perspective to sensitive individuals seeking refuge from the pressures of modern society.

4. Physical Exercise: Engaging in regular physical exercise not only benefits one's physical health but also has profound effects on emotional well-being. Activities such as jogging, yoga, or weightlifting release endorphins—natural mood lifters—and reduce stress hormones, promoting a sense of calm and balance. Exercise offers a constructive way for sensitive men to channel their energy and emotions, improving both their physical and mental health.

In essence, self-care practices provide sensitive men with the tools they need to navigate their emotional landscape with confidence and resilience. By embracing mindfulness, journaling, creative expression, spending time in nature, and prioritizing physical exercise, men can embark on a journey of self-discovery that celebrates their sensitivity and promotes emotional well-being.

Unveiling Your Strengths: A Personal Journey of Discovery

Embracing sensitivity isn't just about recognizing its value; it's also about understanding how it manifests uniquely within each individual. As we embark on this journey of self-discovery, let's delve into the empowering process of conducting a strengths inventory to unveil the hidden treasures within our sensitivity.

1. Understanding Your Emotional Landscape: Begin by reflecting on your emotional responses to various situations. What emotions do you frequently experience, and how do they influence your actions and interactions? By identifying your emotional triggers and patterns, you gain valuable insight into your emotional landscape.

2. Recognizing Patterns of Sensitivity: Explore recurring themes in your life where sensitivity plays a significant role. Are there specific contexts or environments where you feel most attuned to your emotions? Pay attention to moments when your sensitivity serves as a guiding compass, leading you towards deeper connections and insights.

3. Identifying Strengths in Vulnerability: Challenge the misconception that vulnerability equates to weakness. Instead, recognize vulnerability as a profound strength—one that allows you to connect authentically with others and cultivate meaningful relationships. Your ability to empathize, communicate openly, and navigate complex emotions is a testament to your inner strength.

4. Embracing Authenticity: Authenticity lies at the heart of genuine social engagement. Encourage yourself to show up authentically in your interactions, expressing your sensitivity without fear of judgment or rejection. By embracing your true self, you create space for meaningful connections and foster a sense of belonging.

5. Setting Boundaries: Remember that authenticity doesn't mean sacrificing your well-being. Set boundaries that honour your needs and protect your emotional energy. Communicate assertively and respectfully; assert your limits when necessary, prioritizing self-care and emotional resilience.

6. Embracing Growth: View your sensitivity as a source of continual growth and self-discovery. Embrace new experiences, challenges, and opportunities for personal development. As you navigate life's journey, remember that every obstacle is an opportunity for growth and empowerment.

7. Celebrating Your Sensitivity: Finally, celebrate your sensitivity as a unique and invaluable aspect of your identity. Embrace the richness of your emotional landscape, recognizing that your sensitivity is not a flaw to be corrected but a strength to be celebrated.

Through this strengths inventory, you'll gain a deeper understanding of your sensitivity and the unique strengths it brings to your life

Key Takeaways

- Redefining Strength: Sensitivity isn't a weakness, it's a sign of emotional intelligence, a crucial predictor of success in life. Embrace your vulnerability as a source of strength.

- Mindset Shift: Challenge the inner critic that labels sensitivity as "unmanly." Reframe sensitivity as a strength and recognize the positive aspects like empathy, deeper connection, and emotional awareness.

- Building Confidence: Express your sensitivity with confidence. Start small in low-pressure situations, practice assertive communication, and celebrate your victories in expressing your authentic self.

- Self-Compassion and Mindfulness: Treat yourself with kindness and understanding. Use mindfulness techniques to observe your thoughts and emotions without judgment, fostering self-compassion and authentic communication.

- Self-Care Practices: Sensitivity can guide your self-care journey. Pay attention to your needs and personalize your self-care practices with activities like meditation, spending time in nature, or creative expression.

- Building Support Networks: Surround yourself with people who create a safe space for vulnerability. Supportive relationships provide a sense of belonging, foster empathy, and combat feelings of isolation.

- Strengths Inventory: Identify your unique strengths associated with sensitivity. Empathy, intuition, and emotional intelligence are valuable assets. Create a living document to track your growth and celebrate your strengths.

- Authentic Social Engagement: Start small and gradually express your sensitivity in social settings. Lead by example, focus on quality connections, and embrace the imperfections that come with vulnerability.

This chapter has been a transformative journey into the power of embracing your sensitivity. You've learned to reframe your mindset, build confidence in expressing yourself, and navigate the world with greater emotional intelligence. Remember, sensitivity isn't a weakness; it's a superpower waiting to be unleashed.

In the next chapter, we'll explore the evolving roles and expectations of fathers in today's society, challenging traditional stereotypes and embracing a more inclusive and nurturing approach to parenting.

Chapter 10: Redefining Fatherhood

My dad wasn't a man of many words, especially about emotions. He was a rock, a steady presence in my life, but expressing feelings wasn't his forte. I became a father myself, and I realized something – I wanted to be different. Sure, I wanted to provide for my kids, be their steady hand, but I also craved a deeper connection. So, I started small. Sharing my excitement at their successes began with tiny victories. The unrestrained whoop when my son finally mastered his bike, a sheepish confession of exhaustion during a marathon diaper change, and yes, even a glistening tear during that animated film about the lost puppy (you know the one). The initial awkwardness, the fear of seeming "unmanly," slowly dissolved. In its place bloomed a garden of genuine connection. My children saw me not just as Dad, but as a whole person, comfortable with the full spectrum of emotions. I shared my excitement at their successes, openly expressing my frustration during a particularly trying bedtime routine. Gone are the days when being a father merely meant providing for the family—a stoic figure shielding loved ones from life's storms. Today, fatherhood transcends these roles, weaving emotional threads that bind families together. Emotional vulnerability emerges as a cornerstone of this transformation. Fathers now recognize that strength lies not only in physical prowess but also in the courage to express feelings openly. The once-impenetrable armour cracks, revealing a tender heart eager to connect with children on a profound level.

This chapter reveals how parent-child relationships transform, emphasizing fathers' key role in shaping family emotions. By challenging outdated stereotypes and embracing authenticity, fathers are forging new paths, fostering environments where emotional expression thrives.

Emotional Vulnerability within Parenting

Dads – the grill masters, the joke tellers, and the unshakeable pillars of support. That's the image that's been ingrained in society for generations. The truth is, the role of fathers is undergoing a beautiful transformation. We're shifting from the stoic stereotype. We're embracing a new model of fatherhood. It's based on emotional intelligence and vulnerability. This might sound counterintuitive, but here's the thing: expressing your emotions isn't a sign of being "soft" on your kids; it's actually a power move that benefits everyone involved.

Dads no longer bear sole responsibility for providing food and discipline. Today, fathers are actively involved in every aspect of their children's lives – from diaper changes to bedtime stories. This shift isn't just practical; it recognizes fathers' impact on children's emotional well-being.

Modern fathers are encouraged to connect emotionally with their children by sharing feelings and vulnerabilities. Research in developmental psychology has consistently shown that children benefit greatly from having emotionally engaged fathers. When fathers are actively involved in their children's lives and provide emotional support, children exhibit higher levels of self-esteem, empathy, and social competence.

Research backs this up. A study published in the Journal of Family Psychology found that children raised by involved fathers experience a range of positive outcomes, including:

- Stronger emotional intelligence: Dads who openly express and manage their emotions create a safe space for their children to do the same. This translates into better self-awareness, empathy, and social skills for kids.

- Improved communication skills: By talking openly about their feelings, fathers' model healthy communication habits for their children. This sets them up for success in building strong relationships throughout their lives.

- Enhanced self-esteem: A father's love and emotional support act as a powerful confidence booster for children. Knowing they have someone they can rely on emotionally fosters a sense of security and self-worth.

The Science of Connection

So, how exactly does a father's emotional vulnerability translate into positive outcomes for children? Here's where the science gets interesting.

Studies by the University of California, Berkeley, have shown that children raised by emotionally engaged fathers have a stronger prefrontal cortex, the part of the brain responsible for emotional regulation, decision-making, and impulse control. In simpler terms, dads who express their emotions are helping their children develop the ability to navigate their own emotional world effectively.

But the benefits extend beyond brain development. Emotional connection creates a sense of security and trust between fathers and children. Imagine your son struggling with a bully at school. Bottling up his emotions could lead to feelings of isolation and helplessness. However, if he feels comfortable opening up to you, expressing his fear and anger, you can offer support, guidance, and a safe space to process his emotions. This fosters resilience, reduces stress, and strengthens the father-child bond.

The Power of Vulnerability in Everyday Moments

Embracing emotional vulnerability doesn't require grand gestures. It starts with the little things – celebrating your daughter's artwork with genuine excitement, admitting you're feeling overwhelmed during a particularly chaotic bedtime routine, or simply sharing a laugh during a movie night.

These everyday moments of emotional connection send a powerful message to your children: "It's okay to feel your emotions, and it's okay to express them." This creates a safe space for your children to explore their own emotional landscape without fear of judgment.

Emotionally engaged fathers play a crucial role in fostering resilience and coping skills in their children. By modeling healthy emotional expression and coping mechanisms, fathers can help their children navigate life's challenges with confidence and resilience. Studies have shown that children with emotionally available fathers are better equipped to regulate their emotions, cope with stress, and form secure attachments with others.

Redefining fatherhood isn't about abandoning tradition; it's about enriching it. By embracing your emotional intelligence and fostering meaningful connections with your children, you're not just being a dad – you're becoming a role model, a confidant, and a source of unwavering support.

Strategies for Emotionally Supportive Parenting

Effective communication skills are the cornerstone of emotionally supportive parenting. As fathers, our ability to communicate openly and effectively with our children lays the foundation for fostering emotional openness and resilience. But what does effective communication entail?

1. Mastering the Art of Communication:

Communication is the lifeblood of any relationship, and the father-child bond is no exception. Here's the good news: you don't need a psychology degree to be a communication whiz. Here are some practical tips to foster emotional openness with your kids:

- Become an Active Listener: This goes beyond simply hearing the words your child is saying. Active listening involves giving your full attention, making eye contact, and acknowledging their feelings. When our children speak, we must listen attentively, without judgment or interruption. This demonstrates that their thoughts and feelings are valued, encouraging them to express themselves freely

- Validate Their Emotions: Ever feel dismissed as a kid when you were told to "stop crying" or "it's not a big deal"? Don't perpetuate that cycle. Let your children know their feelings are valid, even if you don't necessarily agree with the source of those emotions. Say things like, "I see you're feeling frustrated," or "It's okay to be scared." Validating your children's emotions doesn't mean agreeing with everything they say, but rather acknowledging and accepting their feelings as valid and understandable. This builds trust and strengthens the parent-child bond.

- Use "I" Statements: This helps avoid blame games and promotes understanding. Instead of saying, "You always make such a mess!" try, "I feel frustrated when toys are left on the floor." This shifts the focus to how their actions impact you, encouraging them to consider your perspective.

- Embrace Open-Ended Questions: "Yes or no" answers won't get you very far. Ask questions that encourage your child to elaborate on their feelings, like "What happened that made you so angry?" or "Tell me more about how you're feeling."

2. Emotional Transparency

Think back to your childhood. Do you remember a time your dad expressed his sadness or frustration in a healthy way? Perhaps it was a heartfelt conversation after a loss, or a moment of vulnerability during a challenging project. These instances, where dads model emotional expression, have a profound impact on children.

Here's how to make emotional transparency a part of your fatherhood journey:

- Normalize the Full Spectrum of Emotions: Let your kids see you experience joy, excitement, sadness, anger, and everything in between. Don't shy away from expressing frustration when necessary.

- Embrace the "Ugly Cry" Moment: We all get sad sometimes, dads included. Don't be afraid to let your children see you tear up during a touching movie scene, or share your worries about the future. This shows them it's okay to feel sad, and that vulnerability is a sign of strength, not weakness.

- Own Your Mistakes and Apologize: We're all humans, and messing up is inevitable. When you make a mistake, be open about it and apologize to your children. This teaches them accountability and the importance of emotional repair in relationships.

- Celebrate Each Other's Victories (Big and Small): Jumping for joy after your son scores his first goal is a no-brainer, but what about acknowledging his progress in mastering his multiplication tables? Let your children see your genuine excitement for their achievements, no matter how big or small.

Moreover, creating a safe space for emotional expression is paramount. Fathers should establish an environment where their children feel comfortable sharing their feelings without fear of judgment or ridicule. Encourage open dialogue, validate their emotions, and reassure them that they are loved unconditionally.

Navigating Traditional Expectations and Pressures

Embracing emotional vulnerability can feel like breaking the mold. One of the primary challenges of traditional fatherhood lies in the deeply ingrained societal expectations placed on men. From a young age, boys are socialized to suppress their emotions, leading to a reluctance to express vulnerability or seek support when needed. This can create a barrier for fathers who wish to forge deeper emotional connections with their children but feel constrained by societal norms.

Let's explore the challenges of breaking away from the stereotype and equip you with strategies to become the emotionally supportive dad you (and your kids) deserve to be.

The Challenge: Redefining Fatherhood

Imagine this scenario: you're playing catch with your son. He misses a throw and gets frustrated, kicking the dirt in anger. What's your first instinct? Do you:

A) Crack a joke to lighten the mood?

B) Offer a pep talk about sportsmanship?

C) Acknowledge his frustration and offer support?

The "ideal dad" stereotype might push you towards A or B. But here's the truth – option C is the most emotionally supportive response. Why? Because it validates your son's feelings and shows him it's okay to experience and express frustration.

But acknowledging your child's emotions can feel unnatural, especially if your own father wasn't exactly a model of emotional expression. It's no surprise, then, that many dads face challenges in breaking away from these traditional expectations. Here are some common hurdles:

- The Fear of Seeming "Soft": Society often equates emotional vulnerability with weakness. But here's the secret: expressing your emotions takes strength, not weakness. It's about being authentic and creating a genuine connection with your children.

- The Pressure to be the "Strong One": Dads are often seen as the emotional pillars of the family. While providing stability is important, it's equally crucial to show vulnerability. Your children need to know it's okay to rely on you for emotional support, not just practical needs.

- The "Boys Don't Cry" Mentality: This outdated idea stifles emotional expression in men from a young age. Breaking free allows you to model healthy emotional expression for your sons. This sets them up for success in their own relationships.

Empowering fathers to overcome societal pressures and embrace a more emotionally present and supportive role involves a multifaceted approach that addresses both internal and external factors. Here are some strategies for fathers to consider:

- Self-awareness: Encourage fathers to reflect on their own beliefs and attitudes towards masculinity and fatherhood. By becoming aware of any internalized societal pressures or expectations, fathers can begin to challenge and redefine their roles in alignment with their values and aspirations.

- Open communication: Foster an environment of open communication within the family. Encourage fathers to engage in meaningful conversations with their children, actively listening to their thoughts, feelings, and concerns. By creating space for dialogue, fathers can strengthen their emotional connection with their children and cultivate trust and understanding.

- Seek support: Encourage fathers to seek support from peers, mentors, or mental health professionals. Breaking away from traditional notions of stoicism and seeking help when needed is a sign of strength, not weakness. By sharing their experiences and challenges with others, fathers can gain valuable insights and resources to navigate their parenting journey more effectively.

- Lead by example: Role-modeling emotional openness and vulnerability is crucial for fathers seeking to embrace a more supportive role. Demonstrate the importance of expressing a wide range of emotions authentically and encourage children to do the same. By leading by example, fathers can create a safe and nurturing environment where emotional expression is valued and encouraged.

- Flexible parenting styles: Encourage fathers to adopt flexible and adaptive parenting styles that prioritize emotional connection and responsiveness. Recognize that there is no one-size-fits-all approach to parenting and encourage fathers to tailor their parenting practices to meet the unique needs of their children.

- Challenge gender stereotypes: Encourage fathers to challenge traditional gender stereotypes and embrace a more inclusive and egalitarian approach to parenting. By actively participating in caregiving tasks and sharing household responsibilities, fathers can model gender equality and demonstrate that nurturing and caregiving are not solely the domain of mothers.

Overall, empowering fathers to overcome societal pressures and embrace a more emotionally present and supportive role requires a willingness to challenge traditional norms, cultivate self-awareness, seek support, and prioritize authentic emotional connection with their children.

Building Emotional Connections with Children

Building emotional connections with children is not just about being physical. It also requires meaningful interactions to build emotional bonds. Spending quality time with children strengthens parent-child bonds. It greatly impacts their emotional well-being and development.

Firstly, quality time entails being fully present and attentive when interacting with children. Put away distractions like phones and work thoughts. Focus only on the child. Engage with genuine interest and enthusiasm when playing a game, reading a story, or having a conversation.

Moreover, engaging in activities that promote emotional bonding is essential. These activities can vary depending on the child's interests and age but should ideally involve opportunities for open communication, shared experiences, and mutual enjoyment.

So, what does quality time actually look like? It's not about passively watching TV together (although that can have its place occasionally!).

Here are some ideas to get you started:

- Get Down on Their Level: Literally! Play games, build forts, and read stories together. These activities create a sense of fun and connection, fostering emotional intimacy.

- Embrace Their Interests: Is your daughter obsessed with horses? Take her to a riding lesson, even if horses aren't your thing. Showing genuine interest in their passions demonstrates your love and support.

- Unplug and Be Present: Put away your phone and silence distractions. Being fully present in the moment allows you to truly connect with your children on an emotional level.

- Make Mealtimes Memorable: Dinner can be more than just refueling. Turn it into a conversation starter, asking your children about their day and sharing your own experiences.

- Embrace Bedtime Rituals: Story time, singing lullabies, and even just a few quiet moments of cuddling before sleep foster a sense of security and emotional connection.

Embracing vulnerability is another crucial aspect of building emotional connections with children. Children learn by example, and when fathers demonstrate vulnerability by openly expressing their emotions, it teaches children that it's okay to be vulnerable and authentic. This fosters an environment of trust and openness where children feel comfortable expressing their own emotions without fear of judgment.

Research has shown that children who have emotionally engaged fathers tend to have higher self-esteem, better social skills, and improved academic performance. Additionally, they are less likely to engage in risky behaviors such as substance abuse or delinquency.

In conclusion, building emotional connections with children through quality time and vulnerability not only strengthens the parent-child bond but also lays the groundwork for their emotional and psychological well-being. By prioritizing these aspects of parenting, fathers can cultivate deeper, more meaningful relationships with their children that last a lifetime.

Promoting Co-Parenting Partnerships

Whether through divorce, separation, or blended families, fostering a healthy emotional environment for your children requires a unique approach. Here's the good news: by prioritizing communication and shared emotional responsibility, you can build a strong co-parenting partnership that benefits everyone involved.

Bridging the Gap: The Power of Communication

Communication is the lifeblood of any successful relationship, and co-parenting is no exception. However, in these situations, communication takes on an added layer of complexity. Here are some strategies to cultivate open and effective communication:

- Beyond the "Handoff": Co-parenting communication extends beyond just scheduling logistics. Schedule regular check-ins to discuss your children's emotional well-being, academic progress, and any concerns you may have. These conversations foster collaboration and ensure a united front when it comes to emotional support.

- Respectful Dialogue, Even in Disagreements: Disagreements are inevitable, but avoid turning communication into a battlefield. Focus on respectful dialogue, even when you don't see eye-to-eye. Remember, the goal is to prioritize your children's emotional well-being, not win an argument.

- Be more concerned about your goals: When communication gets heated, remind yourselves why you're doing this—for the emotional and psychological well-being of your children. This shared purpose can help navigate difficult conversations and keep you focused on what truly matters.

Your daughter returns home from school devastated after a fight with a friend. She longs to talk to you but hesitates. She's unsure if your response will be like the one from her other parent. In this kind of scenario, she will mostly prefer to speak to her mom before thinking about her dad.

Presenting a unified approach to emotional support with your co-parent creates security and consistency for your children. They can express themselves freely without fear. Conflicting responses or emotions are not a concern. Here's how to move beyond potential conflict and establish a united front:

- Focus on Shared Goals: Despite potential disagreements, remind yourselves that you both share the same ultimate goal – the emotional well-being of your children. Keeping this "why" at the forefront helps navigate challenging conversations and fosters collaboration.

- Develop a Communication Style: Work with your co-parent to establish a communication style that feels comfortable for both of you. This might involve regular check-ins, utilizing a co-parenting app, or simply agreeing on respectful communication even during disagreements.

- Embrace Transparency: Keep each other informed about your children's emotional state, any concerns you might have, and any upcoming events or milestones. This transparency fosters a sense of partnership and ensures a cohesive approach to emotional support.

Beyond Communication: Sharing the Emotional Load

Communication is crucial, but the real magic happens when you and your co-parent actively share the emotional responsibility of raising your children. Here are some ways to ensure your children feel supported, regardless of where they are:

- Quality Time, No Matter the Distance: Make the most of your time with your children, even if it's limited. Be fully present, actively listen to their concerns, and offer emotional support. Technology can be your friend — utilize video calls to connect when you're apart.

- Consistency is Key: Work with your co-parent to establish consistent routines and expectations regarding emotional support. This might include bedtime rituals, communication norms regarding emotional outbursts, and positive reinforcement strategies.

- Celebrate Milestones Together: Did your son finally conquer his fear of stage fright during the school play? Celebrate his achievement, even if you weren't there in person. Express your pride and acknowledge his effort — this fosters a sense of unity and security.

- Embrace Different Parenting Styles: Acknowledge that you and your co-parent might approach emotional support differently. Focus on finding common ground and respecting each other's parenting style, as long as it creates a safe and nurturing environment for your children.

Key Takeaways

The traditional expectations of fatherhood are evolving. Society is recognizing the importance of emotional connection and vulnerability in dads.

- Emotional Intelligence Matters: Dads who are emotionally intelligent raise children who are better equipped to manage their own emotions and build healthy relationships.

- Breaking Free from the Mold: Challenge societal pressures to conform to a rigid definition of masculinity. Embrace your full emotional range to be a more present and supportive father.

- Quality Time is Key: Invest in quality time with your children, creating a space for open communication and emotional bonding. It's not about the quantity, but the emotional connection you build.

- Vulnerability is Strength: Sharing your emotions with your children models healthy expression and creates a safe space for them to do the same. Don't be afraid to show your tears or laughter.

- Embrace the Full Spectrum: Let your children see you experience joy, sadness, anger, and everything in between. Suppressing emotions sends the wrong message.

- Validate Their Feelings: Acknowledge your children's emotions, even if you don't necessarily agree with the source. Say things like "I see you're feeling frustrated" to show you understand.

- Open Communication is Vital: Talk to your children about their day, their feelings, and their worries. Practice active listening and create a space where they feel comfortable sharing openly.

- Co-Parenting Partnerships Thrive on Communication: Work with your co-parent to establish clear communication and shared emotional responsibility, ensuring a unified front for your children.

- Embrace the Journey: Redefining fatherhood is a continuous process. Reflect on your experiences, celebrate your victories, and seek support when needed. You are not alone on this path.

Redefining fatherhood involves embracing emotional vulnerability, challenging traditional norms, and fostering deeper connections with children. By empowering fathers to embrace their authentic selves, we can create healthier family dynamics and nurture happier, more resilient children.

Conclusion

The Road Ahead

I'm happy that you made it to the end of this book. We explored masculinity deeply in this book. We have uncovered the layers of men's "hidden struggle." You've seen the power of vulnerability in building connections and leading emotionally. You learned emotions, explored workplace dilemmas, and deconstructed traditional masculinity.

We explore emotional vulnerability in men. This challenges conventional beliefs and embraces authenticity. Each chapter guides us to understand ourselves and our relationships better.

Now, you stand on the precipice of this newfound awareness. Imagine a life where:

- **Your partner** feels truly seen and heard. You openly communicate your needs and desires. This builds a deeper connection based on trust and emotional intimacy.

- **Your children** thrive in an emotionally safe space. You model healthy emotional expression. They can navigate feelings confidently.

- **Your workplace** transforms into a collaborative haven. You foster trust, respect, and belonging among your team.

- **You** experience a profound sense of self-acceptance. You embrace all facets of your emotional being, no longer afraid to show the world the authentic you

As we conclude this exploration, let's reflect on the insights gained and the road ahead.

Embracing Vulnerability: Men often suppress feelings due to societal expectations, which causes internal turmoil. This can lead to isolation. We shed light on this silent struggle. This is the first step to breaking free from emotional repression. It's time to liberate ourselves from the shackles of societal expectations and embrace our authentic selves.

The Power of Vulnerability: We explored the transformative power of vulnerability. Embracing vulnerabilities helps us connect deeply with others and be authentic. We have seen how vulnerability sparks personal growth and meaningful relationships through stories and research. Let's remember that true strength is being vulnerable and authentic. It leads to a fulfilling life.

Navigating Relationships: We explored how open communication, empathy, and understanding foster intimate partner connections. Embracing vulnerability in relationships creates trust, intimacy, and support. Let's commit to showing up authentically and vulnerably in our relationships. This will nurture the bonds that enrich our lives.

Mastering Emotional Intelligence: Emotional intelligence is crucial for success at work and in leadership roles. Integrate these principles into our professional lives, creating collaborative environments where everyone thrives.

Masculinity is Redefined: Traditional notions are deconstructed. This paves the way for a more inclusive definition. It is also more compassionate. Let's challenge outdated stereotypes and embrace the diversity of masculine identities.

Fathers can redefine fatherhood by prioritizing emotional connection and support. Let's lead by example, fostering resilience, empathy, and authenticity in the next generation. Armed with knowledge, self-awareness, and empathy, we can navigate life's challenges gracefully. We are equipped to handle difficulties with resilience. Continue building emotional intelligence, practicing self-care, and embracing vulnerability for strength.

Here are ten points encompassing the strategies needed for success:

1. Self-awareness: Understand your emotional landscape and recognize when you're experiencing internal struggles

2. Courage to be vulnerable: Embrace vulnerability as a strength, allowing yourself to authentically express emotions

3. Effective communication skills: Learn to communicate openly and honestly in relationships, fostering understanding and connection.

4. Emotional literacy: Develop the ability to recognize and articulate emotions, enhancing self-awareness and empath.

5. Emotional intelligence in the workplace: Cultivate emotional intelligence to navigate professional challenges and foster collaborative workspaces.

6. Leadership skills: Acquire leadership qualities such as empathy, resilience, and authenticity to inspire and motivate others

7. Creating a supportive environment: Foster psychological safety and trust within teams to encourage collaboration and innovation

8. Challenging societal norms: Challenge traditional notions of masculinity and embrace vulnerability as a source of strength

9. Embracing sensitivity: Recognize the strength found in sensitivity and vulnerability, both personally and in relationships

10. Reimagining fatherhood: Redefine fatherhood by prioritizing emotional connection, support, and authenticity in relationships with children

By incorporating these tools into your life, you can navigate the complexities of emotional vulnerability, foster meaningful relationships, and thrive personally and professionally.

Now is the time to take action. Commit to living authentically. Embrace vulnerability. Champion emotional expression in ourselves and others. Together, we can create a world where sensitivity is celebrated and emotional well-being is prioritized.

As we embark on the road ahead, let's remember that true strength lies in our ability to be vulnerable, to connect deeply with others, and to live authentically. May this journey lead us to a life filled with meaning, fulfillment, and genuine human connection.

Key Takeaways

- Emotional vulnerability is a strength, not a weakness: Throughout the book, we've emphasized that embracing vulnerability allows for authentic connections and personal growth.

- Effective communication is paramount in all relationships: Whether in personal or professional relationships, open and honest communication fosters understanding, trust, and empathy.

- Traditional masculinity is evolving: We've explored the limitations of conventional masculinity and highlighted the importance of redefining societal norms to promote inclusivity and emotional expression.

- Emotional intelligence is essential for success: Cultivating emotional intelligence enables individuals to navigate challenges, lead effectively, and foster collaborative environments.

- Workplaces thrive on collaboration and emotional support: Creating a culture of collaboration and emotional support enhances productivity, innovation, and employee satisfaction.

- Leadership requires emotional authenticity: Effective leadership is grounded in authenticity, empathy, and vulnerability, inspiring trust and motivation in teams.

- Self-awareness is key to personal growth: Understanding and accepting your emotions and vulnerabilities is fundamental to personal development and meaningful relationships.

- Sensitivity is a source of strength: Contrary to societal norms, sensitivity is a strength that fosters deeper connections, empathy, and resilience.

- Fatherhood is about emotional connection, not just provision: Redefining fatherhood involves prioritizing emotional presence, support, and engagement in your children's lives

- Authenticity breeds fulfillment: Ultimately, embracing emotional vulnerability and authenticity leads to more fulfilling relationships, personal well-being, and a more inclusive society.

By internalizing these key takeaways, you can navigate the complexities of emotions, relationships, and societal expectations with greater confidence, resilience, and authenticity.

This book, "Emotional Vulnerability in Men," has provided you with invaluable tools and insights to embrace vulnerability as a source of strength and navigate life's challenges with authenticity.

As we conclude this enlightening journey together, remember that your journey towards emotional growth and self-discovery is ongoing. Embrace each moment as an opportunity for growth and connection.

I believe in you! You have the power to cultivate meaningful relationships, lead with empathy, and live a life filled with purpose and fulfillment.

I hope this book has been helpful to you. If you have any questions or need further support along your journey, please don't hesitate to reach out. I am here to support you every step of the way.

If you found this book helpful and transformative, please consider leaving a review on Amazon. Your feedback will not only inspire others to embark on their own journeys of self-discovery and emotional growth but also motivate us to continue creating meaningful books that empower and uplift.

THANK YOU

Thank you for choosing "Emotional Vulnerability in Men." Your support and interest in this book mean the world to me.

I poured my heart and soul into crafting this guide to provide expert insights and practical strategies to help you uncover your authentic self and achieve personal growth. I hope that you have found the content valuable and empowering.

As an independent author, your feedback and review on the platform where you purchased the book would be immensely valuable. By sharing your thoughts, you help me grow as a writer and also assist others in discovering the transformative power of emotional vulnerability.

Your support fuels my passion for writing and motivates me to continue creating content that resonates with you and addresses your needs.

To leave a review please click below

Richard Garraway Author Page

Thank you for investing in " Emotional Vulnerability in Men."

With heartfelt appreciation,

Richard Garraway

References

Levant, R. F. (2020). The Tough Standard: The Hard Truths About Masculinity and Violence

American Psychological Association (APA). (2021). Speaking of Psychology: Men, masculinity, and mental health, with Ronald F. Levant, EdD2

Daniel Goleman - Emotional Intelligence https://www.amazon.com/Emotional-Intelligence-Matter-More-Than/dp/055338371X

The Center for Creative Leadership: https://www.ccl.org/

Creating a Psychologically Safe Workplace: https://hbr.org/2023/02/what-is-psychological-safety

Emotional Intelligence 2.0 by Travis Bradberry and Jean Greaves

American Psychological Association: https://www.apa.org/monitor/2018/

Weakness vs Vulnerability - What's the difference? (2023, November 23). WikiDiff. https://wikidiff.com/weakness/vulnerability

Ms, M. T. (2012, August 29). 3 Myths about Vulnerability. Psych Central. https://psychcentral.com/blog/3-myths-about-vulnerability#1

Waling, A. (2018). Rethinking Masculinity Studies: feminism, masculinity, and Poststructural Accounts of Agency and Emotional Reflexivity. The Journal of Men's Studies, 27(1), 89–107. https://doi.org/10.1177/1060826518782980

Jharrelson. (2023, July 13). Exploring traditional masculinity definitions and societal impacts - Unmasking Masculinity. Unmasking Masculinity. https://unmasking-masculinity.com/blog/exploring-traditional-masculinity-definitions-and-societal-impacts

Men: A different Depression. (2005, July 14). https://www.apa.org. https://www.apa.org/topics/men-boys/depression

GGI Insights. (2024, February 22). Gender Roles: Navigating the Dynamics of Societal Expectations. Gray Group International. https://www.graygroupintl.com/blog/gender-roles

Pittenger, C., & Duman, R. S. (2007). Stress, Depression, and neuroplasticity: a convergence of mechanisms. Neuropsychopharmacology, 33(1), 88–109. https://doi.org/10.1038/sj.npp.1301574

Kulsum, Z. A., & Sinha, A. (2023). Gender Stereotypes, Societal Pressure and Emotional Expression among Men. ResearchGate. https://doi.org/10.25215/1103.194

Gould, W. R. (2023, March 7). Why vulnerability in relationships is so important. Verywell Mind. https://www.verywellmind.com/why-vulnerability-in-relationships-is-so-important-5193728

Vulnerability: Definition & Tips. (n.d.). The Berkeley Well-Being Institute. https://www.berkeleywellbeing.com/vulnerability.html

Romero, L. E. (2023, September 12). The power of vulnerability in leadership: experts say authenticity and honesty can move people and achieve results. Forbes. https://www.forbes.com/sites/luisromero/2023/03/08/the-power-of-vulnerability-in-leadership-experts-say-authenticity-and-honesty-can-move-people-and-achieve-results/?sh=3c39f9645ef7

Psychreg, & Psychreg. (2023, November 21). Understanding your emotions is the first step to emotional wellness. Psychreg. https://www.psychreg.org/understanding-your-emotions-first-step-emotional-wellness/

KaraMcD. (2022, April 11). 8 Benefits of Being Vulnerable that will Improve your Life. https://myquestionlife.com/benefits-of-being-vulnerable/#:~:text=8%20Benefits%20of%20Being%20Vulnerable%20that%20Will%20Drastically,8%208.%20Opens%20us%20up%20for%20growth%20

Happimynd | Read blog. (n.d.). HappiMynd. https://happimynd.com/blog/masculinity-and-mental-health-breaking-down-societal-expectations#:~:text=Societal%20expectations%20of%20masculinity%20often%20dictate%20that%20men,leading%20to%20increased%20stress%2C%20anxiety%2C%20and%20even%20depression.

Moore, M. (2022, October 11). The good kind of vulnerability. Psych Central. https://psychcentral.com/relationships/the-good-kind-of-vulnerability

Leo. (2023, October 19). What is Trust in Relationship? Exploring the Key Elements of Building Strong Bonds - Psychologily. Psychologily. https://psychologily.com/what-is-trust-in-relationship/#:~:text=Trust%20is%20the%20foundation%20of%20a%20healthy%20relationship.,to%20establish%20a%20strong%20bond%20with%20our%20partner.

Creating love in the lab: The 36 questions that spark intimacy. (2015, February 12). Berkeley. https://news.berkeley.edu/2015/02/12/love-in-the-lab/

Presence. (2022, August 23). Why the Vocabulary of Emotions is Critical to Emotional Intelligence. Presence. https://presence.com/insights/why-the-vocabulary-of-emotions-is-critical-to-emotional-intelligence/

Robinson, L. (2024, February 5). Effective communication. HelpGuide.org. https://www.helpguide.org/articles/relationships-communication/effective-communication.htm

Rcc, P. S. M. (2023b, December 11). The power of I statements: Communicating effectively. Well Beings Counselling. https://wellbeingscounselling.ca/the-power-of-i-statements/#:~:text=Key%20Takeaways%3A%201%201%20statements%20focus%20communication%20on,conflicts%2C%20%20providing%20feedback%2C%20and%20strengthening%20relationships.%20More%20items

American Management Association. (2023, January 26). The Five Steps to Conflict Resolution. American Management Association. https://www.amanet.org/articles/the-five-steps-to-conflict-resolution/

MSEd, K. C. (2022, December 11). Utilizing emotional intelligence in the workplace. Verywell Mind. https://www.verywellmind.com/utilizing-emotional-intelligence-in-the-workplace-4164713

Ferebee, A. (2023, April 5). Battle of Emotions: Why men fight for feelings and what they can do to open up - Knowledge for men. Knowledge for Men. https://www.knowledgeformen.com/why-men-fight-for-feelings/

Carli, L. L. (2001). Gender and social influence. Journal of Social Issues, 57(4), 725–741. https://doi.org/10.1111/0022-4537.00238

Dovbysh, A. (2024, January 6). The art of emotional intelligence: 12 strategies for mastering your emotions. Ideapod. https://ideapod.com/the-art-of-emotional-intelligence-12-strategies-for-mastering-your-emotions/

Emotional intelligence in Leadership: Why it's important. (2019, April 3). Business Insights Blog. https://online.hbs.edu/blog/post/emotional-intelligence-in-leadership

Panchal, R. (2024, March 5). What is Emotional Leadership? Leading with Empathy And Compassion. Theleaderboy.com-Leadership Advice For Smart Leaders. https://theleaderboy.com/what-is-emotional-leadership/

Hcsuper. (2022, November 29). Daniel Goleman's Emotional Intelligence Theory: Explanation and Examples | Resilient Educator. Resilient Educator. https://resilienteducator.com/classroom-resources/daniel-golemans-emotional-intelligence-theory-explained/

Thompkins, S. (2023, August 28). Emotional intelligence and leadership effectiveness: bringing out the best. CCL. https://www.ccl.org/articles/leading-effectively-articles/emotional-intelligence-and-leadership-effectiveness/

Team, C. (2023, October 15). Leadership styles. Corporate Finance Institute. https://corporatefinanceinstitute.com/resources/management/leadership-styles/

Coursera. (2024, February 19). Collaboration in the Workplace: Benefits and Strategies. Coursera. https://www.coursera.org/enterprise/articles/collaboration-in-workplace

González, C. (2023, June 19). Keys to foster a culture of open communication in the company. Team Insights. https://teaminsights.io/en/blog/news/keys-to-foster-a-culture-of-open-communication-in-the-company/

Iacoviello, V., Valsecchi, G., Berent, J., Borinca, I., & Falomir-Pichastor, J. M. (2021). Is traditional masculinity still valued? Men's perceptions of how different reference groups value traditional masculinity norms. the Journal of Men's Studies, 30(1), 7–27. https://doi.org/10.1177/10608265211018803

BetterHelp Editorial Team. (2024, February 22). Exploring effects of the APA's "Traditional masculinity" on men and boys

| BetterHelp. https://www.betterhelp.com/advice/mental-health-of-men-and-boys/why-does-the-apa-call-traditional-masculinity-harmful-to-men-and-boys/

Bjelland, J. (2023, December 13). Embracing sensitivity: The Crucial role of Self-Acceptance for Highly Sensitive people — Julie Bjelland. Julie Bjelland. https://www.juliebjelland.com/hsp-blog/embracing-sensitivity-the-crucial-role-of-self-acceptance-for-highly-sensitive-people

Borelli, J. L., Smiley, P. A., Gaskin, G. E., Pham, P. T., Kussman, M., & Shahar, B. (2019). Children's and Parents' Perceptions of Vulnerability as Weakness: Associations with Children's Well-Being. Journal of Child and Family Studies, 28(10), 2727–2741. https://doi.org/10.1007/s10826-019-01453-1